AROUND *A* GREEK TABLE

AROUND A GREEK TABLE

Recipes & Stories

ARRANGED ACCORDING TO THE LITURGICAL SEASONS OF THE EASTERN CHURCH

KATERINA KATSARKA WHITLEY

Photographs by Jasmin Hejazi

LYONS PRESS

Guilford, Connecticut

An imprint of Globe Pequot Press

*Dedicated to the Katsarka clan
and all those who joined their lives with ours*

Lyons Press is an imprint of Globe Pequot Press.

Photo on p. viii by Niki Craig.
Text design: Maggie Peterson
Layout artist: Maggie Peterson
Project editors: Gregory Hyman & Meredith Dias

Library of Congress Cataloging-in-Publication Data

Whitley, Katerina Katsarka.
  Around a Greek table: Recipes and stories arranged according to the liturgical seasons of the Eastern Church / Katerina Katsarka Whitley ; photographs by Jasmin Hejazi.
    p. cm.
  ISBN 978-0-7627-7836-2
1. Cooking, Greek. 2. Food habits—Greece. 3. Orthodox Eastern Church—Liturgy. 4. Cookbooks.
I. Title.
  TX723.5.G8W45 2012
  641.59495—dc23

2011035836

Printed in the United States of America

10 9 8 7 6 5 4 3 2 1

Contents

Acknowledgments

How far back may one go to give credit for nurturing and for showing that cooking is more than a daily chore? I will start with my grandmother, who kept us all together in her self-effacing manner, and my own mother, who left us too soon but whose memory is connected with some cherished images of her in the kitchen; and my stepmother, who also was a fine cook despite limited facilities. These three women showed me that caring for one's family is a great calling and that cooking for others is a ministry: *Do all things as unto the Lord,* St. Paul taught us. I want to thank my sister Doritsa who took over when our mother died and became a superb cook and mother in her own right, and my sister Niki who surprised us all with her flair for the finest in cuisine and entertaining. And my brother's wife, Soula, who entered a family of cooks to contribute her own excellent traditions in creative and tasty meals. These three beloved sisters gave me enthusiastic support for this book. To my nieces—Natassa, Lydia, and Phoebe—who entered into the venture of offering and suggesting recipes with gusto, my thanks with my love. And to all my Greek clan with whom I have broken bread through the years—many thanks for the meals and, above all, for the singing.

I especially remember the first editors who liked my food essays and published them: at the *News and Observer,* Garnet Bass, and my wonderful editors at the *Christian Science Monitor* in the 1980s. Thanks go to my agent, Kathleen Davis Niendorff, for believing in the project and my editor, Katie Benoit, for her enthusiasm and care with details. And special thanks to Eleni Melirrytou and the women of St. Barbara Greek Orthodox Church in Durham, North Carolina.

Above all to my own family, especially my husband, Rudy, who never complained as I learned and experimented, even in my days of ignorance in the kitchen, and my lovely daughters, Niki and Maria, who brought friends home to taste my cooking, and later their husbands and children. It is for the sake of these beloved and delightful children and grandchildren that I have written this book of Greek memories and recipes. "Everything Mika cooks is filled with goodness," my second grandson, Jeremy, said. What can be a higher accolade?

Preface

I learned Greek history around our kitchen table. Together with the taste and smell of lemony sauces and the evocative flavor of onions and tomatoes sautéed in olive oil, I absorbed my father's stories of the Balkan wars, of World War I, of man's greed and treachery, of deprivations and courage. I also ingested a strong national pride together with oregano and cumin. I learned of my father's original hometown in a land now Turkish and, though I've never visited it, I can still see it as he painted it with words, sharing with me the flavors of the place he loved. His mother hailed from fabled Constantinople—the Polis, as the Greeks proudly called it, still yearning for it in the middle of the twentieth century—and from that place she brought to us the memories and tastes of rich Anatolian cooking.

At our table met the east and west of Greece. The Katsárka clan from Adrianople and Constantinople were from the east, but my mother, with the ancient and fateful name of Persephónê, came from the west, from mountainous Epirus, bringing with her a hint of all the tragedies associated with the murderous Ali Pasha. She, an orphan, was taken from her hometown at four years of age, and the only memory she shared with us from that place was a sound she heard as a child—the creaking of the watermelons as they grew and expanded in the fields. The east and west met in Thessaloniki, and there the children of the union were nourished with stories as much as with food.

So together with recipes from my family and my own strong inclination to incorporate Greek flavors in new ways, I offer here stories and recipes of survival and simplicity in the midst of hard times; of earthy vegetable flavors that honor the soil that produced them; of meat and fish cooked with imagination; of legumes that contribute to good health; and of abundance and festivity that surround holidays.

Around a Greek Table: Recipes Served with Flavors, Aromas, and Stories

*C*ooking was something my mother did. My father's contribution to the kitchen was that he did most of the buying, especially poultry and fruit, and sliced the freshly bought bread for the main meal of the day. Mothers did not work outside the home when I was a child, so they spent much of the morning preparing for the main meal. Most everything they needed was available from vendors in the street. The woman was in charge of the kitchen then. My brother, Kostakis, expected to be waited on by his three sisters, and we spent much of our childhood being furious with him. Things have changed, of course, and now he waits on his wife and cleans up after she does the cooking. How nicely some things improve, even in old countries. As children, we girls helped by chopping nuts for baklava or by pouring the lemon juice as mother whipped *avgolémono* sauces. The rest of the time we were at school, or we studied, practiced the piano, or involved ourselves with the church gatherings that provided our only entertainment. There was a firm conviction in our unusual Greek household that children's lives should not be burdened by household chores. Our schoolwork and play came first. The duties of adult life would arrive soon enough; for now, we were to excel in our studies. So I didn't learn to cook while at home. I observed, absorbed the cooking aromas, and ate the food provided.

Our immediate household had another peculiarity. Though we were Greeks, we must have appeared strange to our fellow citizens because we belonged to a tiny group known as Protestántes. In Greek Orthodox parlance that meant either weird or not completely Greek. The Orthodox church year honors hundreds of saints; we considered that all Christians were saints, according to St. Paul, who, after all, had visited Thessaloniki and had established the first Christian *ekklesía* there—a congregation of believers. We considered ourselves direct descendants in the spirit. Our clan observed only the major holidays together with the rest of the Greeks: Protochroniá (New Year's Day), Easter, and Christmas. But the rest of the world had distinct celebrations during Epiphany and wild partying during the Carnival that preceded Lent, cleansed themselves on Clean Monday (just before Lent), fasted in a peculiarly Greek manner during the forty days of Lent, and had unending feasting during the day and week of Easter. On May Day (Protomayiá), it was lovely to see wreaths adorning every balcony on the street—except for ours, how embarrassing! My father, ever mindful of the dangers of idolatry, associated the May Day ritual with ancient practices, so we had to avoid it. August fifteenth commemorated the Virgin Mary in ways that would be unthinkable to her modest village upbringing. This was our life. We observed, we enjoyed, but we did not fully participate in the life of the world surrounding us. Years later, after coming to the United States to study, I thought we Katsarkas would have felt more at home among the evangelicals in the American South than we did in Thessaloniki.

Yet we did have some common ground with all Greeks: we shared the same customs in cooking and a similar devotion to family and clan. We possessed the added distinction of having a very close community of friends, because our clan was large and the church community so small that we found our entertainment and support among ourselves. Sometimes the Orthodox seemed a mystery to us; other times we envied them their fun; most of the time we were content to have our own company enlivened by eating and playing together.

Even though our apartment was very small, our mother was hospitable and the guests who passed through the city—especially Brits and Americans who shared the Protestant faith—were welcomed around our Greek table. The main meal of the day was in the early afternoon, and we always ate it as a family, with or without guests.

The Greeks observe a different timetable for meals, and even the language reveals the difference. Breakfast is practically nonexistent: hot tea, toast, cheeses, and marmalade seem to be enough for those who do eat breakfast. The concept of noon begins at two o'clock instead of twelve and lasts through nearly five o'clock, especially in the summer. So when a Greek says, "Come for a meal at *mesiméri*" (midday), this can mean any time between two and five o'clock. The traditional hour for the main meal of the day is three. Then comes the siesta and, in the Greek lexicon, afternoon comes *after* five o'clock, when the siesta ends. Eating out at night starts well after eight o'clock, closer to ten for the partygoers; life and lights continue in the cities and the villages through the night. For those who eat at home, fruit, yogurt, cheese, and bread seem sufficient.

This is how we grew up—in community and in simplicity. As in every other country, Greek habits have changed drastically in the past fifty years; with more money and prosperity there is more luxury, together with more complexity in cooking, more of the developed world's illnesses, more partying, drinking, and additional worries about the loss of family solidarity, and the loss of the strict morality that used to be imposed on the youth of the land. Some things are better and others are much worse.

Yet there are recognizable Greek characteristics that remain: the strong ethos of hospitality—always involving food and eating—and the family ties that are not easily broken. My sister-in-law has the whole family in for Sunday dinner after church, year round; my younger sister and her husband built a lovely villa that includes their own apartment and two separate apartments for their two children and their families. They will never feel lonely.

When you are invited to a Greek home, expect to be fed. When you drop in, you will invariably be offered a drink and something to eat. Food is an indispensable element of Greek hospitality and history. When the shipwrecked Odysseus is taken home by the lovely Nausicaa, he is not asked questions; he is bathed and dressed, and then invited to a banquet. No one knows who he is, but he is still treated like an honored guest. He must eat before he is asked any questions. I love this Greek heritage of hospitality. May it long continue around Greek tables.

I was already a young mother living in California when I remembered that Greek cooking had once been important in my life. I had lived in the States since I was sixteen and had forgotten it. Then one morning as I walked in the yard of our rented house in Monterey, I came across a bed of flat-leaf parsley. (I thought the curly parsley I had seen up to then as decoration on plates was a kind of joke. There was no smell and no taste to it.) I now bent down and snipped a couple of tender shoots. The smell hit me, making me dizzy with remembered meals. I broke it with my teeth and tasted it. With tears stinging my eyes, I returned to the kitchen and thought, "I must make *keftédhes*." From then on I started remembering Greek smells and tastes, and the memories led me to rediscover my Greek heritage and the riches of its kitchens. In this book you will learn some of the secrets of Greek cookery and hear the stories that are told around Greek tables in the honored tradition of combining myths with food.

Ritual, the Liturgical Seasons, and This Book's Arrangement

I came to a profound appreciation of ritual rather late in my life, as I started anew in the United States. Being far from my family created a vacuum that I filled first by participating fully in the academic rites of my colleges and later by creating rituals for my young family in my new country. Family rituals are almost always connected to meals or bedtimes and are embellished by storytelling. For some, they are substitutes for a religious experience; for others, they are closely tied to their faith. Religion is bound up with ritual, and eating together is a ritual. The Greek Orthodox Church culture that surrounded my childhood years has deeply entrenched and beloved traditions. Many of our highly educated friends in Greece tell us that they are not believers but that they love the rituals of their church; therefore they stay within its embrace.

In addition to having a long history, Greek culture is inextricably linked to Orthodoxy, whose liturgical calendar lends order to lives that otherwise would be chaotic. Life in Greece tends to be volatile, exuberant, and disorganized. It's comforting and orderly to have designated church seasons that make it possible to feel secure by repeating customs and eating meals that have historic significance.

When I decided to collect my recipes and essays to write a book on Greek food, I found it inevitable that I would follow the liturgical calendar and that I would connect the recipes to its elegant frame.

I start with Easter because it means new life and a new beginning. (And, yes, the churches consider the first day of their calendar to be September 1, but I hope I will be excused for choosing the greatest of all festal days—Easter Sunday—for this beginning.) Not all the recipes in this book are associated with a particular church season, but many are, and I name those with a liturgical or traditional connection and give the stories behind them. For each church season I add other recipes that would enhance the tradition by offering complete meal choices from starters and salads to main dishes, sides, and desserts. Not all of us eat the same kinds of food in Greece, but the order of this book will give you a fairly accurate idea of what is cherished as having religious or ritual meaning and what has been regionally created and loved. Throughout the book I have interwoven essays on culture, history, myth, and family ritual.

The main and ritually observed church seasons that I use to frame this book are: the Easter season, which is the fifty days from Easter Sunday to Pentecost; the Pentecost season, which lasts until Advent; the Advent season, which in the Orthodox Church begins on November 15 and lasts until Christmas Day; the Twelve Days of Christmas, counted from December 25 to January 5; Theophany (Epiphany in the West), which in Greece is celebrated for three days, January 5–7; the Great Sarakostí, or the Forty Days (Lent in the West), a period that starts with Clean Monday and has moveable dates that depend on the date of Easter; and finally Holy Week, the week that leads to Easter Sunday, when the great cycle begins all over again.

I must emphasize that the Eastern Church has many feast and fast days during these long liturgical seasons. Saints are cherished and honored with their name days, but most feasts are associated with the Virgin Mary or the life of Christ. I focus on the most important ones in this book.

A Gentle Disclaimer

These are cultural and culinary stories, not theological or religious ones. I have used the liturgical calendar as a frame because it has an order that appeals to me and that has affected Greek cooking for generations. However, because the Orthodox Church calendar focuses more on fast than feast, as a writer of recipes I am singling out not the many fasting periods of the church but the great feast days and the seasons that follow them. Since the Orthodox Church doesn't observe seasons as much as saints' days and fasts, I use the seasonal names as they are recognized in the wider Christian community, most notably for the seasons following the day of Pentecost and for the preparation that leads to Christmas, known as Advent.

About Greek Recipe Titles and Pronunciation

The Greek language is phonetic, so you pronounce all the syllables and vowels. I have placed accents on the words, because this is where English speakers have the greatest difficulty. In English the tendency is to throw the accent to the beginning syllables of words: the Greek Socrátes becomes Sócrates, and Aristotélis becomes Aristotle, and so on. In Greek words the stress is most often on the ultimate (last) or penultimate (next-to-last) syllables. Hence the accents on the final syllables of *baklavá*, *halvá*, and *moussaká* and the penultimate of *saláta*, *tzatzíki*, and *dolmádhes*. There are some consonants that don't exist in Greek, like *j* and the soft *g*, together with the *sh* and *ch* sounds, and there are some Greek consonants that cannot easily be replicated by one born to English. The letter chi (Χ, χ), for instance, is more pronounced in the Greek than the English *h* but less than the English *k*, rather like what Scots say in "lo*ch*"; in the recipe names I have transcribed χ as *h*. The third letter of the alphabet, gamma (Γ, γ), is nearly impossible for other speakers to duplicate at the beginning of a word, as in the Greek *gala*, milk; to show that it is more guttural and yet not harsh, I have written it as *gh* in the recipe names. There are many words in Greek that use the letters delta (Δ, δ) and theta (Θ, θ). Delta is pronounced as a voiced *th* as in "this" and "that"; I have written the voiced *th* as *dh*. Theta is pronounced unvoiced as in "think"; I have shown that simply as *th*. All vowels are open in Greek. I hope this will help you when you are reading this book and when you visit the country itself. The Greeks will be appropriately impressed.

Sourcing Greek Ingredients

Some of the recipes In this cookbook feature imported ingredients that may not be carried by your local supermarket. Many of them can be found at fine grocery stores or shops specializing in Greek foods, and *all* ingredients utilized in this book can be easily found on the Internet. Because of its wealth of Greek and Balkan food products, my pre-ferred website for sourcing Greek ingredients is Parthenonfoods.com. They offer quick and reliable service and are responsive to queries and refund requests. A quick Internet search will also reveal myriad additional options.

Easter Bread
(*Lambrópsomo/Tsouréki*)

Easter Soup
(*Mayirítsa*)

Fig and Walnut Salad
(*Saláta me Sýka*)

Romaine Lettuce with Vinaigrette
(*Maroúli Saláta me Ladholémono*)

Green Peas in Sauce
(*Arakás me Sáltsa*)

Cheese Pastries
(*Tyropitákia*)

Oven-Baked Lamb with Potatoes
(*Arní toú Foúrnou*)

Lamb on the Grill
(*Païdhákia*)

Baklavá

Apricot Phyllo Flutes
(*Floyéres me Verýkoko*)

Apple and Nut Phyllo Flutes
(*Floyéres me Mílo*)

Chapter 1

EASTER DAY

*I*n theological language, Christians are called Easter people. Yet one cannot recognize the joy of Easter unless one has gone through the dark of Good Friday's sorrow. Easter *Sun*day would have no meaning without the dark of Passion Week—the Great Week, as the Greek Orthodox call it. The saddest day of the week is Great Friday, the terrible day of death. All over the country, the mournful pealing of church bells prepares the populace for the solemnity of the day. On and on they ring their deep adagio song of death, commemorated that night with the Epitáphios, the symbolic bier of the dead Christ, being carried from neighborhood to neighborhood, to the main square of the village, and finally back to the church. The bier is followed by a procession of clergy and acolytes with only candles for light. In the cities, people stand on their balconies holding candles and making the sign of the cross while the bier passes below. On Great Saturday the bells continue their mournful dirge. Near midnight the churches fill so that the people may receive the new light of resurrection while "Christós anésti" (Christ is risen) is being proclaimed by the priest. The bells ring at midnight in a crescendo and accelerando of joy to lead us to Easter Sunday, Anástasis.

☙ THREE WORDS FOR EASTER ❧

Anástasis means Resurrection and the word finds its honored place both in the church calendar and in ordinary Greek usage as Easter Sunday. A substitute for "Anástasis" is "Lambrí," which means the brilliant one, the shiny, glorious day, most often used by the people of the countryside. The most familiar word, however, is "Páscha," from the Hebrew for Passover. It is indeed a brilliant day and a moveable feast. Easter Day in the Orthodox Church depends on the moon cycle, as it does in the Western Church, but the Greek date is still determined by the Julian calendar, while the Western is fixed by the Gregorian calendar. So sometimes the two fall on the same date, but in most years Orthodox Easter is a week later, and occasionally it's as late as a Sunday in May. Together with Easter Day and because of it, Ascension, celebrated on the fortieth day and the following Sunday, and Pentecost, the fiftieth day—both great holy days—are also moveable. The other festal days are fixed.

On Easter Sunday the weather is always beautiful, the churches are adorned, and, unlike on other Sundays, they are full, starting with Holy Week and continuing in the week following. It is the greatest religious holiday in Greece, beloved by all—not necessarily for its religious significance in a now highly secular country but because it is so deeply ingrained in the Greek culture.

The meadows bloom with unnumbered wildflowers, those humble but oh-so-beautiful little flowers that bless a land that is more arid than lush. The aromas of herbs and flowers make one dizzy with happiness and well-being. *Anástasis* is happening all over the land, and the people rejoice. They have fasted, more or less, during the Lenten season, and they are now ready to enjoy food in all its tastes, flavors, and ethnic significance. The celebration starts at midnight on Great Saturday, the last day of Holy Week. The priest emerges at midnight with the light in his hands to proclaim, "Christós anésti," and the people cry out, "Alithós anésti" (He is risen indeed). And an ancient canticle proclaiming this truth in the elegant Greek of ages past is sung over and over again by the congregation waving its candles and spilling into the large courtyard of the church. The people crack one another's red eggs, repeating the resurrection words, and then they go home to eat *mayirítsa* soup, the Easter bread called *tsouréki*, and boiled eggs. Central to all this is also the Christian understanding of the baking and breaking of the Bread (see page 5).

Easter Bread

Lambrópsomo/Tsouréki

Tsouréki is a Turkish word that came to Greece with Asia Minor Greeks. The main Greek name is *lambrópsomo*, the bread for Lambrí, Easter Sunday. The traditional Easter meal, which is centered on this bread and also includes a soup, is served immediately after the Saturday night church service to break the long fast of Lent (Sarakostí). This recipe makes enough delicious bread to share with family and friends.

Makes 10 loaves

1. In a large mixing bowl (about 15 inches in diameter), dissolve the yeast in 1/2 cup warm milk (around 110°F). Add 1/2 cup sugar and 1 cup flour. Mix well, cover, and put in warm place to proof. My mother's generation used wooden tubs that looked like small bathtubs for this dough and covered it with blankets.

2. Meanwhile, heat the butter with the remaining 1 1/2 cups milk and 2 cups sugar over very low heat until butter melts. Let these liquids then come toward room temperature.

3. In a medium bowl, mix 2 cups of flour with the citrus peel and *mahlépi*; set aside. Put the eggs in another bowl with the salt and beat for a couple of minutes.

4. Now check the yeast; it should be covered with bubbles. Add 2 cups of the flour mixture to it; stir and mix thoroughly. Check the melted butter liquids for temperature. If they are at or below 110°F, you are ready to use them. Add 2 more cups of flour to the yeast mixture and blend well. Mix in half of the melted butter liquids, then the beaten eggs, then more flour, then the rest of the liquids. Keep adding flour until you have a dough consistency you can work with, not too sticky. Turn it out onto a lightly floured work surface and knead it until satiny.

5. Sprinkle the dough generously with flour, then divide into two large mixing bowls. Cover and let it rise until the dough doubles in size, about 2 hours. Uncover, turn one at a time onto the work surface, punch, cover again, and let them rest a few minutes.

6. Line four baking sheets with parchment paper or simply grease them well. Tear off about a cup of dough and roll it into a long rope, about 1 inch in diameter. Repeat with another handful of dough. Form a loaf by braiding three of these dough ribbons. Repeat the

Ingredients

3 tablespoons yeast

2 cups milk

2 1/2 cups sugar

10–12 cups flour (I use about half unbleached and half all-purpose white)

2 sticks unsalted butter

Zest of an orange or lemon

2 teaspoons ground *mahlépi* (see note 1)

6 eggs, plus 2–3 yolks for brushing on loaves

Pinch of salt

Blanched almond halves for topping

Red eggs, for a really Greek bread (see note 2)

process to form additional loaves. For other designs, try a figure 8 or a spiral—the possibilities for lovely designs are many.

7. The dough shapes will become much larger, so place them on the baking sheets leaving lots of room for expansion. Parchment paper works very well. Cover with clean, dry kitchen towels; let them rise to at least double their size; then brush with beaten egg yolks that contain a few drops of cold water. This will give them that lovely shiny color. Decorate with almond halves; brush these with the egg wash also so that they stick to the dough. In the center of the loaves, place a red egg, if you are so inclined.

8. Let the loaves rest while you preheat the convection oven to 350°F or regular oven to 375°F. Bake them for 45 minutes or until the tops become deep red or reddish brown. I like to slide them off the baking sheet onto the oven rack for a few more minutes. The bottom should sound hollow when they are fully baked. Place on racks to cool. You will be amazed at how marvelous your kitchen will smell.

9. This bread is puffy with a soft interior but can be sliced easily when cooled. Let the loaves cool completely before wrapping. They keep well, and the flavor increases; they also freeze well. You may want to slice and toast them on following days for more aroma and a different texture.

Note 1: Mahlep or mahlab, or *mahlépi* in Greek, is a Middle Eastern spice made from pulverized cherry pits that's perfect for *tsourékia* (plural). It is available in Middle Eastern markets and on the Internet. Some cooks dissolve the *mahlépi* in boiling water and use the liquid essence of the aromatic. You can approximate the flavor at home by simmering 3 cloves, 1 bay leaf, and 1/2 stick cinnamon in 3/4 cup water for 20 minutes; strain and use 2 teaspoons of this liquid for each teaspoon of *mahlépi*.

Note 2: For true *tsourékia* presentation you need really red eggs; you can find the Greek egg dye on the Internet. Follow the directions on the dye package; these eggs are not boiled before dyeing and are for show only.

Easter Soup

Mayirítsa

Connie Phillipson, a British nutritionist living in Greece, wrote extensively on Greek diet during the first decade of this century. I enjoyed her columns because she asked questions similar to my own: How did the people who created the first combinations of food-stuffs reach their astounding conclusions? How did the first people who devised this particular soup—with no knowledge of nutrition at that time—know that the *mayirítsa* was the perfect nourishment for those who had fasted for forty days?

The Lenten fast avoided meat and dairy products, leaving a vegetarian diet that was poor in iron, especially at a time of no supplements and artificial vitamins. Phillipson says that *mayirítsa* is indeed the ideal food to break the fast. This soup is a traditional cornerstone of the meal, but it would not be easy to reproduce in an American kitchen, because its base comes from the entrails of the Paschal lamb—heart, liver, spleen, lungs, and intestines. I give here an alternative recipe, without the entrails but still *mayirítsa*.

3 pounds lamb shoulder and bones

1 whole onion, scored through, peeled

2 stalks celery with leaves

1 carrot, peeled

2 tablespoons olive oil

5–6 scallions, whites and about 1 inch of dark green, cut into small rings

10 lettuce leaves, cut into slender ribbons

1 cup rice

1/4 cup chopped parsley

1/4 cup chopped dill

3 egg yolks, at room temperature

Juice of 1 lemon, or more, to taste

Serves 8

1. Place lamb, onion, celery, and carrot in 3 quarts of cold, salted water and bring to a boil, then simmer for a few hours, until meat is very tender. Strain broth into another pot. Discard bones and vegetables; cut the meat into small pieces and add to the clear broth.

2. In the oil, sauté the scallions and lettuce slightly; add rice and stir to coat.

3. Add sautéed greens with rice to the broth and simmer until rice is tender. Add the parsley and dill (this soup likes lots of dill). Just before serving, bring broth to heat again. Whip the egg yolks, then slowly add the lemon juice, beating until frothy. To prepare the yolks for the heat, dip a ladle of soup from the pot and add it to the egg mixture in a steady stream while beating. Repeat, and stir this into the soup so that it all heats through. Do not boil. Taste for seasoning, and serve immediately.

Bread as a Symbol and a Reality

In the Christian tradition, the great mystery centers on the breaking of the bread, the sacrament of the Holy Eucharist. The word Eucharist comes from the Greek word for thankfulness, *euharistía*, which etymologically reveals the state of blessedness and grace. This most sacred service to believers is the reenactment of the broken body of Christ on the cross. "The body of Christ, the bread of heaven," the priest intones as the bread is shared with the faithful. Denominations differ on the frequency of the experience and on the wine, with many choosing grape juice and little glass vials instead of wine and the common cup favored by the liturgical churches: Orthodox, Roman Catholic, Anglican/Episcopal, and Lutheran. But the disagreement rarely extends to the bread and its essence—the mysterious yet evident, the earthy yet heavenly substance.

Bread. What is more common in the experience of humanity? When I first returned to Greece after a lengthy initial residence in the States, I tried to explain to my father the difference between Americans as I saw them then and the Greeks as I knew them. After I gave my father examples of both generosity and waste as practiced in my new country, he reached for a bread metaphor. "They are more innocent, naïve," he concluded, "because they haven't had to sweat for their bread through innumerable centuries of occupation and starvation, as we have." (Well, yes, all things do change.) I think of this universal essence of bread as I mix the yeast with warm water and sugar. I wait for it to proof and offer a prayer that a hunger for justice will start bubbling, proofing, around the world. The evidence of "proof," when I uncover the yeast, is present in the countless bubbles that are now ready to burst open. Then I bury this live yeast in mounds of flour and other earthy substances. I knead it and pray that all good things will find fruition in our world. That after the burying of the yeast, resurrection will happen in the rising of the dough. It cannot fail, I think, as I look at the daffodils that are being liberated from the soil to lift their lovely yellow heads to the sun. A few hours later I look at the results of my covered yeast and dough and sigh with contentment. The dough is pushing upwards, lifting the towel that is covering it, ready to burst forth like liberation and resurrection. The spores of yeast have been liberated and the dough has come alive.

For me, baking bread at home is both a corporal act of mixing and kneading and a spiritual practice of prayer and hope. When the bread is cut into pieces to be given to the congregation, we call it the Breaking of the Bread. In the Eastern tradition it is called Artoklasía, which means the same. But the Orthodox also have special seals made by monks which, when stamped on the *prósphoron* (the bread baked for Holy Eucharist), remind one of the centuries-old traditions of the church. The seals contain a cross with, in its four quadrants, the Byzantine letters IC/XC/NI/KA, for *I(esou)s Ch(risto)s nika*, or "Jesus Christ conquers." These letters are stamped on five loaves that are placed on the altar.

The Easter bread that Greeks make to be consumed outside the church, regardless of their denomination or affiliation, is now called *tsouréki*. It is beautiful to look at and delicious to eat. In my home we ate it mostly for breakfast, and Mother made enough loaves to last for weeks. Because we are Greeks, we do not have uniformity in the recipe, something you will notice throughout this book. Each one of us eventually finds her personal way of making *tsouréki*. I finally settled on this recipe because it reminded me of what I had eaten as a child. I hope you try it, until it becomes your own. With modern yeasts and excellent flours you cannot fail.

Fig and Walnut Salad

Saláta me Sýka

For the majority of Greek Orthodox, Great (or Holy) Saturday ends with the midnight church service, followed by soup, bread, and eggs. Sleep comes long after midnight, so the main Paschal meal arrives quite late on Easter Sunday, and it invariably includes lamb. Here tradition ends. All the additional dishes for the Paschal meal depend on regional and family customs. In my home, for instance, the Paschal meal came after Sunday morning worship, an early afternoon meal that was sufficient for the day. In this chapter I offer some supplementary choices for the festal day before I come to the main act—the lamb.

Here is an elegant salad for a special day.

Serves 6

1. Preheat the oven to 350°F. Roast the walnuts on a cookie sheet for about 10 minutes.

2. Remove the tiny stems from the figs, slice them open without cutting through, and, if they are dry, soak them in orange juice while you prepare the rest. (I like the Greek dried figs bought through the Internet; there are good dried figs from Turkey available in the markets.)

3. Wash, drain, and arrange whole lettuce leaves on a salad platter, fanning them out. Overlay them with the darker green of spinach. Arrange figs and walnuts on top.

4. In a bowl or jar, combine mustard and salt. Add oil, vinegar, and honey, and mix well. Spoon over the salad before serving.

For the salad:

1/2 cup walnut halves

12 fresh figs, in season, or Greek or Turkish dried figs

2 cups orange juice (if using dried figs)

Romaine lettuce and baby spinach

For the honey dressing:

1 teaspoon dry mustard

1 teaspoon salt

4 tablespoons olive oil

3 tablespoons balsamic vinegar

1 tablespoon honey

Romaine Lettuce with Vinaigrette

Maroúli Saláta me Ladholémono

3 romaine lettuce hearts

16 or more Kalamata olives

4 hard-boiled eggs

2 scallions

1/4 cup olive oil

3 tablespoons balsamic vinegar

2 basil or mint leaves, torn really fine

1 tablespoon snipped parsley

1 tablespoon snipped dill

This salad, more traditional than the preceding fig and walnut salad, is a fine choice to accompany a full meal like the Paschal dinner.

Serves 8

1. Rinse and spin romaine hearts, then lay them on a cutting board and cut crosswise into 1/4-inch-wide strips. Spread on a platter. Arrange olives around and on the lettuce. Peel the eggs (you might as well take advantage of all those boiled Easter eggs), slice each lengthwise into 4 wedges, and arrange on top. Wash and slice the scallions and disperse them over the salad.

2. Whisk together the oil and vinegar until the mixture becomes cloudy. Add the basil or mint, parsley, and dill. Mix well and spoon over the salad. You will be surprised at the taste of boiled eggs when anointed with *ladholémono*. (*Ladholémono* means oil with lemon, but you may also add any herbs you like in the liquids.)

Green Peas in Sauce

Arakás me Sáltsa

Vegetables as side dishes were rare in the country of my childhood. Instead, they usually were the whole meal—very healthy and tasty. Now that Greeks eat more meat and poultry than in the past, this dish may be served as a hot or cold accompaniment. When you eat them cold in the summer, place some yogurt on the side and eat them together.

Serves 6

Heat the oil in a 2-quart pot and sauté the scallions until translucent. Add the tomatoes; stir and sprinkle the sugar over them. Add the peas and 1/2 cup water to this sauce. (Omit the water if using frozen peas.) Check frequently that the peas aren't burning. Season with salt and pepper, and cook, partially covered, over medium heat. When the peas are almost soft, add the dill and parsley. Allow all the water to be absorbed, so that the peas remain in a rich red sauce.

1/2 cup olive oil

5–6 scallions, cut fine

2 large peeled tomatoes, chopped with their juice, or 1 14.5-ounce can diced tomatoes

1 teaspoon sugar

1 pound shelled fresh English or garden peas (if unavailable, use frozen, not canned)

Salt and pepper, to taste

1/4 cup snipped fresh dill

1/4 cup snipped fresh parsley

❧ ALL ABOUT PHYLLO ❧

Phyllo, the flaky, feather-light pastry that is the glory of Greek baking, finds its place in every part of the meal. From savory cheese- or meat-filled appetizers, through imposing entrees like the chicken pie called *kotópita* and the vegetarian's mainstay spanakopita, to the legendary syrup-drenched baklava, phyllo's paper-thin layers are the building blocks of Hellenic dining pleasure. Success does come with practice, but phyllo baking requires only patience and the courage to try until you master the handling of it. Like all worthwhile crafts, you will find it easier each time. Greek music by Theodorakis playing in the background helps!

Phyllo dough now is available from many grocery stores and websites and comes in different thicknesses: thin and thick or peasant (*horiátiko*); it comes with various dimensions also. The most readily available is the Athens-brand phyllo that now is packaged in two separate airtight cylinders of paper-thin sheets of dough, with twenty sheets in each roll, measuring approximately 14 x 9 inches. You can use one cylinder and leave the rest in the freezer until needed. But to work successfully with the dough, I recommend that you take care to bring it to room temperature. This is where most would-be bakers fail. It is not enough for it to thaw; it must stay wrapped and on the kitchen counter for several hours to become soft and pliable.

Because it is rolled so thin and has little fat in it, phyllo will dry out if exposed to air for any length of time. Until you learn to work fast, keep the dough covered with a damp dishcloth after you open the plastic bag. And be sure not to open it until you have all the other ingredients ready to use.

You will need a pastry brush to paint the sheets of phyllo with melted butter. When building a stack of sheets, you should move along briskly. Now, please, take note: You don't have to cover every inch with butter; it would take forever and it's unnecessary. Just use quick strokes, paying attention to the edges.

After brushing the top sheet thoroughly with butter, score it halfway to the bottom in the shapes you prefer, then wet your fingers with cold water and just flick them all over the pastry. This keeps the edges from curling. After baking, enjoy the results of your effort—phyllo pastries please all the senses.

Cheese Pastries

Tyropitákia

Tyropitákia are midmorning snacks for people going to work, usually without breakfast, or for city people out on a stroll who stop for a rest. All bakeries and shops sell them, hot and delicious, and they are also readily found at the kiosks of street vendors. I offer them usually as an appetizer or accompaniment to a drink. They may also accompany a salad. I must confess that when I want to impress someone, this is what I serve as a first course. The pastries take a little time to prepare, but they are more than worth the effort. They may be prepared ahead of time, and frozen for baking when needed.

12 ounces feta, rinsed in cold water

2 heaping tablespoons sour cream, or 3 tablespoons heavy cream

1 egg, lightly beaten

1/4 cup finely snipped fresh dill weed, loosely packed

1 1/2 sticks unsalted butter

1/2 pound phyllo

Makes 20 *tyropitákia*

1. For the filling, crumble the feta into very small pieces in a bowl; add the sour cream (or, for a much lighter texture, heavy cream), egg, and dill; mix gently. The consistency should be thick and creamy but not watery; you want it firm enough so it will not ooze out as you fold the phyllo around it. You may adjust by adding more feta for firmness or more sour cream for creaminess.

2. Preheat the oven to 350°F. Melt the butter.

3. Before working with the phyllo, please see advice on its handling, page 14. On a work surface, unwrap the phyllo, placing the butter, the filling, and a cookie sheet at hand. With the stack of phyllo before you, butter half of the top layer, fold it in half, butter this and fold it in thirds lengthwise, resulting in a strip of phyllo with five layers of thickness. Butter the top layer. At one end of this long strip, place a teaspoonful of filling. Lift a corner and fold the dough diagonally over the filling, and then proceed to fold the resulting triangle over and over (5 times) as you would do with a flag, until you are left with a neat triangular packet, about 2 inches on a side. Butter the edges and place on the cookie sheet with the fold on the bottom. Continue this process until all the phyllo has been used up. (I practiced with paper until I mastered this technique; you may want to do the same.)

    (At this stage, the pastries may be covered well and frozen, if being prepared in advance. I bake them straight from the freezer, covered in foil for 15 minutes and then 30 additional minutes uncovered.)

4. If you are ready to bake, place in the preheated oven for about 20 to 30 minutes. The pastries turn a lovely reddish gold color and fill the kitchen with an irresistible aroma.

❧ EASTER LAMB ❧
CENTRAL TO THE EASTER MEAL AND CELEBRATION

In springtime, symbols take on paramount importance, and they are all around me. I cut the hyacinths from the yard, their fragrance reminding me of Greece with a sweetness that is akin to ache, and they speak to me of myths and age-old customs, like the flowering of the Cross on Easter Sunday and fresh May wreaths hanging from every balcony in Greek cities. I look at the egg and contemplate its self-contained reality, the beginning of life, the renewal of life. The traditional red of the Easter egg has many meanings, but this particular folk tale has been around in the villages of Greece for centuries: When early in Christian history the news of the Resurrection spread, so the story goes, people shrugged it off as impossible. A woman who had just filled her basket with eggs from her coop stood talking with her neighbors about the news. "Bah," she said, in the Greek negative, gesturing toward the eggs. "Could the white turn to red?" And lo and behold, the eggs turned red! A thoroughly non-Christian magic, but oh so familiar to the Greeks.

The most significant symbol of all in this season is the lamb. A symbol of Passover/Easter, lamb is central to both the Hebrew and the Christian stories. It's interesting that there is no religion that rejects lamb in its diet, and still a peculiar fact that in North America the consumption of this meat is rather rare compared to beef and pork. But lamb is central in the Greek tradition, which goes back thousands of years.

Sacrificial in the Hebrew tradition, the symbol of the lamb becomes even more crucial and truly beautiful in the Christian story. What is more stirring than "Behold the Lamb of God," as sung in the leaping octaves of Handel's *Messiah*?

A subtle differentiation in words occurs here in the Greek language. The word *Amnós* refers only to Christ as the Lamb of God; for all the other uses of lamb the word is *arní* or more tenderly, *arnáki*. (So if you have studied ancient or koiné Greek, be sure you ask for lamb in the modern usage of *arnáki* when you visit Greece.)

Arnáki. That's the only kind the Greeks would think of eating at Easter. This is lamb. The rest is mutton, and the Greeks don't like mutton. The difference has to do with age and what the animals eat. The Easter lamb is always milk-fed, and therefore very young. The lambs are born by the thousands between January and March and cared for by shepherds. The only grass the Easter lambs are allowed to eat are the tender new sprouts of the herbs, and these flavor the flesh with a delicacy unknown elsewhere. The shepherds bring them into the villages and towns just before Easter, festooned in ribbons. According to Greek Orthodox tradition, no meat is eaten during the forty days of Lent by the observant. So the lambs are ready, and the people are ready for them.

There are probably as many ways to roast lamb as Greek individuality allows. In an old Athenian cookbook I counted twenty-eight recipes for lamb, each one with a different vegetable. I would like to tell you how the village Greeks do it, so that when you visit the country and smell the enticing roasting aroma filling the atmosphere, you will know how it is created. Many homes in villages, especially of the islands, still have those whitewashed beehive ovens that are found in ancient lands. The fire for the Easter lamb must burn a whole day to heat the oven for the roasting. The heat is produced by burning pine and other special wood with a distinctive aroma; then, after the lamb is placed in the oven, all the cracks are sealed as it roasts slowly overnight.

A more popular way is to roast it over a pit of charcoal in the ground. Again pine twigs are added for the aromatic smoke. A spit with a crank holds the lamb quite high so that it doesn't burn. The fire has to be specially arranged, stronger in the parts that reach the legs and shoulders. Someone turns the spit and bastes the lamb. It takes about three hours to roast outdoors. In many villages, a whole street is dedicated to this activity. Hot charcoal lines the pavement; the spits, loaded with as many lambs as their length allows, extend from one side of the street to the other. Men sit on stools on both sides to turn the spits as required. Women look after the men and offer slices of cheese to passersby. Wine or beer encourages the men to keep the spits turning. It's worth a trip to Greece during Easter just to see this sight. I recommend Arahova near Delphi.

In America, you may try to gather friends in the yard to replicate the method on a small scale. Be sure you baste the lamb frequently. Keep a pan handy for the drippings and for basting. In the basting sauce you should have plenty of lemon and herbs like thyme.

Oven-Baked Lamb with Potatoes

Arní toú Foúrnou

2–3 cloves garlic, or more to
taste

1 4–6 pound leg or shoulder
of lamb, or several lamb
shanks

1 tablespoon rosemary

1 lemon, halved

Salt and pepper

1 bay leaf

4 tablespoons butter, melted,
or olive oil

6 potatoes, peeled and cut
into quarters

2 heaping tablespoons tomato
paste (optional), diluted in
1/2 cup warm water

1 tablespoon oregano

Arní toú foúrnou is a great choice for the main dish during the Paschal season. It was the traditional Easter meal of my childhood and
remains a staple of Greek cuisine.

Serves 6–8

1. Grease a large baking pan. Preheat oven to 375°F.

2. Peel garlic and cut cloves into slivers. Wash meat and pat it dry.
   With a sharp knife open a few gashes and push the garlic cloves
   and slivers deep inside them; do the same with the rosemary.
   Place meat in center of pan, rub with lemon halves, season with
   salt and pepper, and place the bay leaf next to it. Baste with some
   of the melted butter or oil and pour 1/2 cup water around the
   meat.

3. Bake in preheated oven for 1 hour, then add potatoes all around
   the meat. Pour the diluted tomato paste (or another 1/2 cup water)
   over the potatoes and sprinkle with the rest of the melted butter or
   oil, juice from the lemon halves, and oregano. Bake 1 hour more.
   Test for doneness, remove bay leaf, correct seasoning, and serve.

Lamb on the Grill

Païdhákia

If you are not spit-roasting your traditional Easter lamb (see preceding pages), the ubiquitous American backyard grill will give excellent results with cuts large or small. Of them all, tender little lamb chops (*païdhákia*) on the bone, grilled in the Greek manner, are my favorite way of eating lamb.

Eat them with your fingers, and the lemon taste and aroma will bless you. I laugh as I remember that when we had British visitors once at home, we worried that we would be embarrassed before them if we ate the chops with our fingers. This is the only way you can enjoy them. (The southerners I live among say this is the only way to eat fried chicken, too.)

1/4 cup olive oil

Juice of 1 lemon, plus more at serving time

1 garlic clove, peeled and crushed

8 lamb rib chops (more if they are small), bone in

Salt and pepper, to taste

1 tablespoon oregano (see note)

Serves 4

1. Whip the oil with the lemon juice and add the crushed garlic. Rub the chops with this mixture, sprinkle with salt and pepper and oregano, and grill them over very hot coals, 3 to 5 minutes per side. A little pink on the inside is just perfect. Then squeeze fresh lemon juice on them before eating.

Note 1: You can have a spectacular Easter lamb by grilling a leg of lamb also. In that case, flavor the lamb by cutting slits here and there and pushing garlic slivers and cloves into them with some sprigs of rosemary. Rub everything with salt, pepper, and oregano and keep basting it with the oil mixture *(ladholémono)*. Simple and delicious.

Note 2: The only oregano I use is dried, never ground. I prefer the Greek kind, which comes on twigs. I simply rub the leaves between my fingers. There are also fine jarred oreganos available in supermarkets. Dried oregano has a stronger flavor and aroma for cooking than the fresh kind.

Baklavá

In Greece traditional sweets like baklavá and phyllo flutes (pages 23 and 25) never follow a meal but are reserved for communal occasions, as when guests arrive later in the day. At an American table, however, baklavá is always welcome.

You will find that this recipe results in a very different sweet from the cloying and heavy product offered in restaurants.

Note: Before working with phyllo, please see advice on its handling, page 14.

Makes 20 pieces

1. Preheat the oven to 350°F.

2. To prepare the filling, grind the nuts finely in a food processor. Place them in a bowl, and add the dry spices with the 1/8 cup sugar. Mix well and set aside.

3. Melt the butter and have it ready in a small bowl next to you, along with a pastry brush and a buttered rectangular baking pan (see note).

4. Open the phyllo package carefully and place the sheets on the counter. Cover them with a damp dishcloth, and start work, without interruption.

5. Pick up one phyllo sheet at a time, place it in pan, and with quick strokes brush it with the melted butter. Repeat until you have used half of the package—10 sheets. (Keep the rest covered.)

6. Now spread the nut mixture over the buttered dough and immediately start covering it with the remaining sheets, brushing each with butter. Make sure you brush the top sheet thoroughly so that it will brown evenly.

7. Take a very sharp knife and score the baklava. You will make cuts, 2–3 inches apart, first diagonally and then lengthwise to create diamond shapes. You will try to score almost to the bottom of the pan so that it will bake well and be ready for its syrup. Dip your fingers in cold water and sprinkle over the top so that the ends will not curl when it bakes. Bake in the preheated oven for half an hour (or longer, because oven temperature varies), until the top turns golden brown.

For the filling:

2 cups crushed walnuts

2 teaspoons ground cinnamon

1/2 teaspoon ground cloves

1/8 cup sugar

2 sticks unsalted butter

1/2 pound phyllo

For the syrup:

2 cups sugar

1 1/2 cups water

1 cinnamon stick

2–3 cloves

1 slice lemon peel, yellow part only, about 2 inches long

8. While it's baking, bring the sugar, water, spices, and lemon peel to a boil, then simmer until the syrup thickens. This is tricky. You don't want it too thin and you don't want it to crystallize, so watch it. For best results, use a thermometer and let it reach 230°F. Then let it cool.

9. Remove the baklava and let the temperature drop to warm. You don't want either the baklava or the syrup to be hot. Warm will do. (This is a point of debate. Those who originate from Asia Minor—chiefly from the beloved Constantinople, Istanbul—have both syrup and pastry hot; the rest have one hot and the other warm. I prefer warm on both so that the chef avoids a mushy baklava.)

10. Now, carefully, pour the syrup over the baked pastry so that it seeps through all the scored cuts. Cover with waxed paper, then tightly with aluminum foil, and let it sit until all syrup is absorbed. Tilt it now and then to make sure it has penetrated the various levels of pastry. At this point, most Greek cooks leave it alone for a whole day before serving.

11. Cutting it and placing it on a platter is something you do carefully. Baklava will last a long time if it is covered. It also can be frozen and served later.

Note: Since packaged phyllo is precut, for this recipe you may want to use a metal pan measuring 13 x 9 x 2 inches or something similar for greater ease. If your pan is smaller, just roll the edges of the phyllo to fit; if larger, adjust by layering and staggering. You will be surprised how forgiving the phyllo is as it bakes. I have found that phyllo bakes better in metal pans than in glass.

Apricot Phyllo Flutes

Floyéres me Verýkoko

Recently I tried this variation and it was such a hit with family and friends that I decided to include it here; it may become your favorite as well. The beauty of this dish is that you may choose to forgo the next recipe's syrup (and thus lots of calories).

Note: Before working with phyllo, please see advice on its handling, page 14.

1 cup finely ground walnuts

1/4 cup sugar

1 teaspoon cinnamon

1/4 teaspoon ground cloves

1 stick unsalted butter

1/2 pound phyllo

1 14-ounce jar apricot preserves

Makes 10 pieces

1. Mix walnuts, sugar, cinnamon, and cloves. Set aside.

2. Preheat the oven to 350°F. Melt the butter.

3. Take two sheets of phyllo, butter the top one, and fold them in two to make almost a square. Butter the top of this square as well. Place a stream of apricot preserves along the edge of the dough nearest you, leaving a 1-inch margin at the bottom and 2 inches at the sides. Sprinkle the preserves with a heaping tablespoon of the nut mixture and then cover the filling by folding the dough over the filling and away from you. Fold the right and left sides of the phyllo to meet in the middle, butter this surface, and roll so that the filling is enclosed in the pastry. Brush with butter and place with the seal down on a baking sheet. Repeat until all the phyllo and filling are used up.

4. Now take a sharp knife and score the top of each flute diagonally three times. Make sure that the finished surfaces are brushed with butter, and bake in the preheated oven for 30 minutes. These are good just as they are.

Apple and Nut Phyllo Flutes

Floyéres me Mílo

One cylinder of packaged phyllo is just right for this strudel-like dessert that is light and aromatic, delicious with coffee or tea.

Note: Before working with phyllo, please see advice on its handling, page 14.

Makes 20 pieces

1. To prepare the filling, grind the nuts finely and place them in a bowl. Peel, core, and grate the apple, add it to the nuts, stir in the sugar and spices, and mix gently but throughly.

2. Preheat the oven to 350°F. Melt the butter and unwrap the phyllo.

3. Take one sheet, butter half of it, and fold it in two; now you have almost a square. Butter the top. Place a heaping tablespoonful of filling along the edge closest to you, leaving a 1-inch margin at the bottom and 2 inches at the sides. Fold away from you one time to cover the filling, then fold in the left and right sides to meet in the middle. Butter this folded dough and start rolling, so that you have a filled cylinder covered at both ends—cigarlike, as they used to say—approximately 2 1/2 inches long and nearly 1 inch thick. Brush with butter and set on a baking sheet, seam down.

4. Repeat until all the dough and filling have been used. Place flutes in preheated oven. After they bake for about 20 minutes, they look lovely and smell wonderful.

5. While they are baking, boil sugar, water, and lemon peel to reach 230°F. The syrup will be thick. Set it aside.

6. Let the flutes and the syrup cool to warm. Pour the syrup into a small pan with sides (I use a 7 x 9 ceramic pan; the syrup just covers the bottom of the pan). Pick up each flute and roll it in the syrup so all sides are coated by it but the pastry does not become soggy. With tongs, gently place the flutes in tightly sealed containers to have ready for a special treat, or remove to a platter for serving.

For the filling:

1 cup crushed walnuts

1 large Granny Smith apple

1/2 cup sugar

1/2 teaspoon ground cloves

1 teaspoon cinnamon

1 stick unsalted butter

1/2 pound phyllo

For the syrup:

1 cup sugar

3/4 cup water

1 strip lemon peel

So What Is Greek Cooking?

Greek cooking is often misunderstood and criticized, especially for the overuse of olive oil and the tendency of Greeks to serve food that is not hot enough. (My answers to these criticisms: Olive oil was cheaper and more readily available than butter, besides being healthier; in a hot climate, without air-conditioning in the summer, the Greeks would not have enjoyed hot food.) Sure, the criticism that Greeks tend to overcook their vegetables is valid, but I think this is changing. And, perhaps most universally, many have limited experience with Greek food, often identifying it only as gyro, Greek salad, and baklava. Yet, given all of this, non-Greeks repeatedly say to me, "Greek food is my favorite!" So what *is* distinct about Greek cooking?

To answer that question, you must know something about modern Greece and understand who we are now. Residents of Western countries know a great deal about ancient Greece but very little about our recent history—that is, since 1821. The Greeks see themselves even today as living under the great burden of history. "How can we possibly live up to the excellence, the brilliance of our ancestors?" is the implied question in all creative endeavors. They have a point: What nation can ever reach the intellectual and artistic heights of the golden age of Athens in the fifth century B.C.?

When in the nineteenth century Greece emerged as a nation after the four-hundred-plus years of Ottoman occupation—a miracle in itself—the new Greeks wanted to be like their ancestors. They adopted an artificial written language of bureaucracy and stodginess called Katharévousa (pure), and Athens aspired to become worthy of being called a European capital.

Before and after the devastation of World War II, there was a strong division between the city Greeks and the villagers—the peasants—when it came to philosophies on food. Many city Greeks scoffed at the simple foods eaten by the villagers, an attitude that was enforced by Nikólaos Tselementés. Tselementés, a Greek, worked as a chef in fancy American and European hotels—the Ritz in New York and the Sacher in Vienna—and was familiar with elegant, elaborate, and complex cooking. In excruciatingly purist Greek, Tselementés wrote a cookbook at midcentury that became the culinary bible for Greek housewives. In fact, when I was growing up, his name entered the language as a word meaning "a cookbook." His theory was that even French cooking was derived from the culinary arts of the ancient Greeks and Romans, and that most of the dishes that were termed Turkish were actually Greek.

Now, it is true that in the third decade of the twentieth century the relations between Greeks and Turks were filled with bitterness and enmity because of the war of 1922 and the tragic population exchanges that resulted, so it was natural that the Greeks of Tselementés's time would want to denounce everything that reminded them of their humiliation. But one has to admit, after four hundred years the occupiers most definitely would have left some imprint on the occupied. So, is it Greek or Turkish coffee? Does it matter?

It is also true that new research on ancient documents and artifacts, both of Greeks and of Romans, is revealing the high sophistication our ancestors reached in the culinary arts, and on the basis of this research, we can indeed claim that a great deal of what passes as nouvelle cuisine is not so nouvelle after all, since the ancients knew it. If we take all this with a great deal of good humor and stop arguing about food origins in a world that is getting more and more intertwined, we will have a delightful time both cooking and eating.

Now, back to the question: What makes Greek cooking distinct? Well, while consumption of meat and poultry was rare—usually only on Sundays—our diet, albeit limited, was healthy. For me, what makes Greek cooking distinct is found in these indispensible ingredients: lemon, olive oil, fresh parsley, dill, oregano, tomatoes, onions, and feta. (Many would add garlic.) For confections: apricots, oranges, almonds, and walnuts, and honey with cinnamon thrown in.

And Greek cooking would not be complete without fresh vegetables: green beans, spinach, dandelion or chicory (*radhíki* in Greek), and dozens of wild greens that grow on the hills. All kinds of legumes, seasonal fruits, and delicious fish from the surrounding seas round out the characteristic ingredients in Greek cooking.

Today, Greeks are beginning to recapture the old ways of cooking, having realized that the islanders and villagers—known worldwide for their nutritionally balanced Mediterranean diet—know something about Greek cooking after all.

A Menu for the Paschal Meal

Easter Soup (*Mayirítsa*) 7

Fig and Walnut Salad (*Saláta me Sýka*) 11

Oven-Baked Lamb with Potatoes
(*Arní toú Foúrnou*) 18

Green Peas in Sauce (*Arakás me Sáltsa*) 13

Fresh fruit

Later, with coffee: Baklavá 21

A Menu for Outdoor Eating

Romaine Lettuce with Vinaigrette
(*Maroúli Saláta me Ladholémono*) 12

Cheese Pastries (*Tyropitákia*) 15

Lamb on the Grill (*Païdhákia*) 19

Fresh fruit

Apple and Nut Phyllo Flutes (*Floyéres me Mílo*) 25

HEALTHY COOKING

In this collection of recipes you will find ways to cook vegetables as the Greeks have done for generations, but with my own adaptations for a lighter diet that is both delicious and beneficial (well, most of the time). After all, we Greeks excel at adaptations. Through the centuries we have absorbed other cultures and then have put our own imprint on so much that today is known as Greek.

Greek Caviar (*Taramosaláta*)

Stuffed Eggs with Ouzo Flavor (*Methysména Avgá*)

Fried Cheese, Plain or Flambé (*Saganáki*)

Eggplant Puree (*Melitzanosaláta*)

Grape Leaves with Rice Filling (*Dolmadhákia*)

Meatballs (*Keftedhákia*)

Individual Savory Pastries (*Bourekákia*)

White Bean Salad (*Ghíghantes Saláta*)

Salt Cod (*Bakaliáros*)

Garlic Sauce (*Skordhaliá*)

Beets with Stems and Leaves (*Pantzarosaláta*)

Leeks with Rice (*Prasórizo*)

Spinach with Rice (*Spanakórizo*)

Cookie Twists (*Koulourákia*)

Sesame Cookies (*Sousamákia*)

Cabbage Salad (*Lahanosaláta*)

Yogurt and Cucumber Dip (*Tzatzíki*)

Meat Pie with Leeks (*Kreatoprasópita*)

Lamb Baked in Paper (*Kléftiko*)

Shredded Phyllo Pastry (*Kadaífi*)

Custard from Asia Minor (the Greek Crème Brûlée)
(*Kazán Dipí*)

Thin Pie (*Ahamnópita*)

Chapter 2

THE EASTER SEASON

In the liturgical calendar, the Easter season extends from Easter Day to Pentecost, which arrives fifty days after Easter Sunday. In the lean years of the mid-twentieth century, most of the city population stayed home to celebrate and rest since schools were out both before and after Easter Sunday. As more prosperity has arrived and city Greeks no longer have to depend on public transport, they have headed for the countryside during the Easter vacation; the hotels fill ahead of time, the museums close, and all that remains for tourists to enjoy are quiet cities. During this holiday, the villages and islands seem to belong solely to the Greeks, who, released from city tensions, try to recapture the feeling of belonging to the land, to drink ouzo and eat *mezédhes* in the shade of a tree or by the seashore.

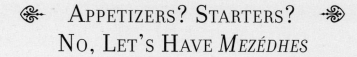

APPETIZERS? STARTERS? NO, LET'S HAVE *MEZÉDHES*

What the tourist notices immediately about Greek tavernas or restaurants is that the appetizers are so tasty and plentiful that a main course is most often unnecessary. Years ago I had the good fortune to eat at a legendary taverna of Piraeus, the port city of Athens. It is the hometown of my younger brother-in-law, and he, a devoted connoisseur of his city, took us to places unknown to tourists. The neighborhood was rather run-down, and the taverna was utterly simple, what today we would call primitive or rustic. The tables were of scrubbed wood and bare, small, with kitchen chairs, the only decoration autographed photos of famous people on the walls. I remember one by Winston Churchill, probably because he had been such a strong presence in my childhood.

My husband had just returned from a year in Vietnam and so, deliriously happy and relieved, we were celebrating. This famous taverna of Piraeus was called Vasílainas, after the owner's surname. In 1920 Mr. Vasílainas had opened a small neighborhood grocery store where he sold nonperishables and wines. His friends would drop in and he would serve them simple appetizers of his own making, the famous Greek *mezédhes*. *Mezé* is the singular, a Turkish word; *mezédhes*, the Hellenized plural. The term *mezédhes* applies to taverna food and picnics; at home, dinners start with "the first plate," which is the first course. They are usually accompanied by ouzo or beer. Little by little, the fame of his *mezédhes* spread, and Vasílainas transformed the grocery store into a taverna. Some of the greats of modern Greek literature—the poets Seféris and Elytis, both Nobel Prize winners—ate there, together with fine actors like the unforgettable Katina Paxinoú, who revived ancient plays.

A big, rather morose-looking man, Vasílainas would serve the diners exactly what he wanted and then he would withdraw to watch from the inner door of his shop. The menu was all *mezédhes*, no entrées. I remember that the *mezédhes* were so many and so generous that I couldn't possibly taste them all, much less eat them. I wish now that, young as I was then, I had had an interest in food, but I had no idea then that cooking would become a passion of mine. But I do remember that everything was perfectly seasoned, and my brother-in-law shared the rumor that if a customer asked for a salt or pepper shaker, Vasílainas would get highly insulted.

Many years later I was sorry to hear that Vasílainas, the taverna, had closed its doors after the death of Vasílainas the man. His grandson has reopened at the same place, to honor the memory of his grandfather, but this reincarnated restaurant has tablecloths, a roof garden, and a limited but full menu.

I mention Vasílainas because his specialty was *mezédhes* and in his taverna they were superb. All restaurants have their own versions, but I will offer here the most traditional and popular of the *mezédhes*; these may be used at any time of the year, in any of the seasons. *Mezédhes* are eaten as a necessary accompaniment to drinking; food must always accompany drink in the country. Ouzo is an aperitif flavored with anise; it's very powerful and everyone drinks it with ice cubes in it, which turn it white, or with ice water. It is drunk in tiny shot glasses. Beer is beloved by Greeks; for nearly a century the Greek beer was the ubiquitous Fix, which disappeared after the 1960s but has recently returned to Greece as Fix Hellas.

Greek Caviar

Taramosaláta

Half a loaf of day-old
  baguette, with crusts
  removed (see note)

1/4 cup taramá

1/2 cup olive oil

Juice of one lemon

Paprika (optional)

Taramá has been called "the poor man's caviar," or "Greek caviar." It's more than that. Taramá is the roe of the carp, which after being cleansed and worked on by experts is sold in jars ready for use in recipes. There are two uses that are quite popular: *taramosaláta* (dip or puree) and *taramokeftédhes* (fried in balls, like meatballs). The use of the word *saláta*, salad, simply means that it has more than one ingredient mixed together. The *taramosaláta* recipe varies according to taste, but here is mine; it results in a creamy, pinkish dip that can serve as the base for a variety of canapés—delicious, for instance, on toasted pita bread or with crunchy fresh veggies and, of course, beer or ouzo. In my home it was the men who enjoyed putting them together.

Makes 12 appetizer portions

1. Soak bread in water. When softened, squeeze the water out. Measure 1 cup of bread mash.

2. Put the *taramá* and the soaked bread in a food processor and pulse until blended. Slowly, while the motor is running, add the olive oil in a steady stream. The *taramá* mixture now will be creamy and light colored. Slowly add the lemon juice and process. Stop the machine, open the top, spoon a bit on bread, and taste. If you want it more creamy, add more oil. *Taramá* itself is quite salty; the bread cuts it down, so add more bread if it tastes too salty.

3. When you are satisfied with the taste, place *taramosaláta* in a bowl and sprinkle paprika on top. It could also be decorated with black olives and parsley. Cover well and refrigerate until ready to serve.

Note: The bread should be Greek, Italian, French, or other peasant-style bread with a substantial texture, not white American.

Stuffed Eggs with Ouzo Flavor

Methysména Avgá

This dish is similar to deviled eggs. The interesting difference in presentation is that these eggs are not arranged on the half shell, like a little boat, but rather on end. You trim each half of the egg so that it can sit like a cup, and then fill that tiny cup. It makes for variety. Ouzo is readily found in liquor stores. These eggs need about a day in the refrigerator for flavors to blend well.

6 eggs, hard-boiled

1 teaspoon ouzo

2 tablespoons mayonnaise

1 tablespoon finely chopped cucumber pickle

2 leaves basil or dill, chopped very fine

Salt and pepper, to taste

Makes 12 appetizer portions

1. Peel the eggs and halve them crosswise. Cut a small slice off each end to make a base, so the egg half will stand up.

2. Remove the yolks and mash with a fork; add the ouzo and blend. Add the mayonnaise and blend well, adding more if needed, depending on the density of the yolks. Stir in the pickle and the basil or dill. Season to taste.

3. Stuff the egg halves and place them on a platter. You can surround them with greens and black olives to create a very pretty effect. You can also add capers on top and create a circle with anchovies around the eggs. There's lots of room for experimentation in this dish.

Fried Cheese, Plain or Flambé

Saganáki me tyri (plain) or Saganáki me gharídhes (flambé)

1 pound Greek *kasséri* or *haloumi* (see note)

Flour for dredging (optional)

1 stick butter

Juice of 1 lemon

Brandy (optional)

The word *saghanáki* does not refer to the cheese but to the "little frying pan" in which it's cooked and sometimes served, particularly in restaurants. You can use a regular-size skillet and cook several slices at once. I use a copper one. This appetizer can become an addiction.

Makes 20 pieces

1. Cut the cheese in slices about 1/4 inch thick and 1 inch wide or larger. Some of us wet the cheese and then dip it in flour. This is not necessary, but it does make the cheese crustier.

2. Melt a little butter in a hot frying pan. Add the cheese and let it heat thoroughly; flip it to the other side. It will begin to melt a bit, releasing an irresistible aroma and crusting on the edges. At this stage, douse with lemon juice and serve.

3. Repeat the process with each cheese slice.

4. Or, if you want to impress, pour some brandy into a cup, pour it on the fried cheese, and light it. Be very careful and keep the bottle away from the fire.

5. Eat the cheese with good bread and ouzo as soon as it begins to cool.

Note: *Haloumi*, a cheese from Cyprus, does not melt when frying, so it's excellent for this meze.

❧ Picnics: A Greek Passion ❧

I grew up at a time when Greece was a poor nation. Everyone was suffering from lack of luxuries, yet it was a good time to be a child. I know that this sounds like an oxymoron, but having to create our own entertainment made us into resourceful adults. There was no television to distract us, no car for Sunday rides, no cinema allowed to the evangelicals of Greece, my own community. I did not see a movie until I was sixteen. Yet we had fun. Most of the memories of those days are interwoven with delicious smells and tastes. In the winter, old men huddled over portable stoves roasting chestnuts; for a few lepta they filled a homemade paper sack full of the hot round balls that warmed our hands as we peeled them. In the summer the charcoal was placed on open, flat stoves to accommodate the ears of corn that were roasting in their green jackets. Again that was a crunchy and good-smelling treat. In fact, until I came to the United States, I did not know that corn was cooked any other way. But the supreme treat in the winter was to go on a picnic. Even though the food was the last consideration for us children, as I look back now I wonder how my mother did it all with no help and how they transported everything without a car.

The Greeks love holidays, and we had many occasions for picnics. The buses and trams would fill with people escaping the city. Our clan's favorite place was the American Farm School, a venerable institution outside Thessaloniki. There we would walk on the unpaved road under the straight poplar trees until we found the perfect spot. For one picnic, we set up on the side of a hillock. One of the adults made a fire in a pit and Mother produced a pretty little bean casserole with a copper cover. We were happy—the last time for us as an intact family before my mother fell ill with what would eventually take her from us. I hold on to that memory, on that hill, on an autumn afternoon. After the food was heated, the women spread a tablecloth on the ground and we ate out of real plates with real cutlery. Then, after we children exhausted ourselves playing, we sat with the grown-ups and sang hymns until twilight started falling and then, quietly, we made ready to return home.

For the city Greek, all restaurant meals are eaten al fresco when weather permits. When urbanites are not able to go to the countryside, a sidewalk or courtyard becomes the locale for a substitute picnic. In the summer, most home meals are eaten on balconies. Some recipes in this section are perfect for eating in the yard or having for a picnic.

Eggplant Puree
Melitzanosaláta

1 1-pound eggplant, or 3 small eggplants weighing 1 pound total

1 heaping tablespoon grated onion

2 cloves garlic, peeled and mashed

4 tablespoons olive oil

2 tablespoons lemon juice

Salt and pepper

A few ground walnuts (optional)

2 tablespoons snipped fresh parsley

You probably know this dish as baba ghanoush. The secret of this recipe is in the smoky flavor of the roasted eggplant. When I go to a restaurant that serves excellent *melitzanosaláta*, I happily return to it, but it is smokiness that makes the difference. If you have a fireplace, you can try burying the eggplants in the hot embers; that's what the old-timers used to do. I have a Vermont Castings stove, so in the winter I drill skewers lengthwise through three small eggplants, open the top of the stove, and suspend them over the fire to give them that intriguing smoky flavor. In the summer you can also place them on the grill over the coals. Whatever cooking method you choose—one of those described above, baking them in the oven at 400°F, or even cooking them in a microwave—be absolutely certain to puncture the eggplants beforehand or they will explode.

This appetizer is a winner. Here is a reliable beginner's recipe; you may want to exercise your creativity later.

Makes 8 appetizer portions

1. Pierce the eggplant and bake or roast by your chosen method until it collapses onto itself. Let it cool, cut off the stem, and remove the skin. If you are lucky, there will be very few seeds; if they are present, try to scoop them out. Mash the eggplant pulp with a fork. You should have about 1 cup mashed eggplant.

2. In a processor or by hand, cream the eggplant with the onion and garlic. Add olive oil; the mixture will become much lighter in color and creamy in consistency. Add the lemon juice and whip. Add 1 teaspoon each of salt and pepper. Taste on a cracker or pita bread. Correct seasoning. Add the ground walnuts, if using, and the chopped parsley, or just use it for decoration on top. Seal well to enhance the flavors; refrigerate. Bring to room temperature before serving.

Note: If you want a stronger flavor, increase the amounts of onion and garlic. I used the minimum amount of oil; you may want to increase that too.

Grape Leaves with Rice Filling

Dolmadhákia

The only large grape leaves I have found in food stores in the United States come in jars and are preserved in brine. If you have a grapevine, try using your own leaves, and enjoy the freshness; they should be the size of an open palm, but tender. Some leaves do tear and others are too difficult to roll, but don't give up.

Makes 80 dolmadhákia

1. The grape leaves found in jars in most major supermarkets are very tightly rolled. Remove each roll gently so the leaves don't tear, and try to loosen them by unrolling the tight cylinder into layers of leaves. Put the leaves in a colander and run cold water over them.

2. Fill an 8-quart stockpot with water, bring to a boil, and drop the leaves in, pressing with a wooden spoon so that the water penetrates among the many layers, for 3–5 minutes. Rinse them again under cold running water. Now spread them on a large platter to cool.

3. In a deep, heavy, and wide pan or Dutch oven (I use a 12-inch steel pan with 2-inch sides), pour 1/4 cup of the oil and sauté the onions until they are translucent. Add the rice and stir to coat. Add the herbs and salt and pepper, cover with water, and let it simmer until all the water is absorbed, or until the rice is almost cooked.

4. Move the rice to a bowl and let it cool.

5. Place both leaves and rice before you at a table, sit down (this will take some time!), put on some Greek music, and start rolling. Lay one leaf on a small clean plate, veins up and shiny side down. If

1 large jar grape leaves

For the filling:

1/2 cup olive oil

1 cup chopped onion

1 cup long-grain rice

1/4 cup chopped flat-leaf parsley

2 tablespoons chopped dill

4 mint leaves, finely chopped

Salt and pepper

2 cups warm water

1 lemon

-AKIA

You will see that the following three recipe names all end in -akia. That's the great gift of the Greek language: you can change any noun to show whether something is big or small, even beloved or disliked. The ending -akia denotes a small size for many of a kind, so dolmádhes is the plural for the regular size and dolmadhákia is the plural for the small size of dolmá, which means something that is wrapped in leaves.

there is a tough stalk, cut it out. Set torn bits of leaves aside. Place 1 heaping teaspoonful of the mixture on the wider edge of the leaf and roll one time away from you as you would a cigarette (who does this now?) or a cylinder. Starting at the bottom, close the two sides of the leaf on top of the filling and continue rolling until all of the leaf is covering the mixture on all sides and you are left with a roll about an inch and a half in length.

6. Place your pan or Dutch oven on a side table. You will have torn leaves left over from the rolling. Line the pan with them, and place the *dolmadhákia* in rows, folded edge down, one next to the other, tightly, until the bottom of the pan is covered. Make another layer on top until all of the stuffed leaves are accommodated.

7. Pour the remaining 1/4 cup oil over them. Pour in enough hot water to barely cover the *dolmadhákia*; add the juice of a whole lemon. Then place an upside-down plate on top of them to keep them snug and intact. (The size of the plate will depend on the size of your cooking pan.) Cover tightly with the pan cover.

8. Bring the mixture to a boil, immediately reduce the heat, and simmer until all the liquid is absorbed, about 1 hour. Take a piece out to test for consistency; if the rice is not done, and the leaves are tough, add some more water and steam again.

9. Serve cold with lemon wedges and slices of feta.

Note: Other recipes call for raisins and pine nuts, but we did not use them at home, and I prefer mine with the rice mixture only. Also, instead of grape leaves, you may use romaine lettuce, but working with it is an even more delicate process.

Meatballs

Keftedhákia

As you will note, Greeks use a lot of ground meat—mostly veal. It was never sold in packages but rather ground in front of our eyes after we chose the right cut of meat. In addition, every family had its own meat grinder at home. Even today I don't buy ground meat pre-packaged but have it ground from a selected piece of meat. For these *keftedhákia* you may use beef, alone or mixed with a bit of pork, or lean ground turkey. The distinctive flavor here is of ground cumin, but Greek flavoring is subtle, not overwhelming.

Makes 30 meatballs

1. Combine all ingredients of the meat mixture in the order given. Mix to form a pliable ball, but do not knead or overmix. Let it rest on counter.

2. In a shallow bowl, place flour for coating and next to it a small bowl with white vinegar. (The vinegar keeps your fingers from getting sticky and greasy, and after you are done, they wash more easily.)

3. In a large frying pan that keeps the heat even, put 1/2 cup olive oil. Dip your fingers In the vinegar and then pinch some of the meat to form a ball the size of a walnut, smaller if you like. Place each ball in the flour and then shake a few at a time to coat them.

4. Heat the oil over high heat and place the meatballs in it, leaving enough space for shaking and turning. You may need to fry them in batches. As the bottom gets crisp, lower the heat to medium and shake the pan or turn the meatballs so that they brown all around. By the time this is accomplished, the meatballs are done through and through. Remove them with a slotted spoon and place on paper towels. When they are cool, you can use them as *mezédhes*. They may also be eaten hot.

For the meat mixture:

1 1/2 pounds extra lean ground meat

1/2 cup dried bread crumbs, or soaked bread squeezed into a pulp (measure it after squeezing the water out)

1 onion, very finely chopped

1/2 cup snipped flat-leaf parsley

1 clove garlic, mashed

1 teaspoon ground cumin

1 teaspoon dried oregano leaves (or tarragon with rosemary, if using turkey)

1 teaspoon salt

1 teaspoon pepper

1 teaspoon ouzo

1 egg

2 tablespoons olive oil

1 cup flour, for coating

1/4 cup white vinegar, for rolling the meatballs

1/2 cup olive oil, for frying

Individual Savory Pastries

Bourekákia

Bourekákia, like *dolmadhákia* and *keftedhákia*, is not a Greek word, but the Greeks, by putting their *-akia* ending on the nouns, have made them theirs. The word is *bourék* in some Arab countries; you will encounter variations of it in several Mediterranean lands and in Turkey. It means that a savory filling is wrapped in some kind of flaky crust. Try experimenting with this dish. My favorite fillings have a feta base, but the combinations are limited only by your own creativity. The dough is excellent; you will be pleased with the results. Though I have to confess that phyllo has a marvelous flaky texture and makes everything look and feel exquisite, these *bourekákia* are so attractive and tasty that you can serve them at the most elegant party. My guests rave about them, and the grandchildren occasionally declare: "Make them like this from now on!" (Credit for this recipe goes to my friend Eleni Melirrytou; I have incorporated just a few tweaks.)

Makes 20 bourekákia

1. First, prepare the pastry: Mix the flour, yeast, and salt. Cut the cold butter into the flour and crumble it up. Add the oil and continue mixing. When the fats have been absorbed by the flour, add the egg and then the yogurt. Mix well and let rest.

2. Combine the filling ingredients, mix well, and set aside.

3. After dough has rested 30 minutes, preheat the oven to 350°F.

4. The dough will now be soft and pliable. Add enough flour to handle it without stickiness. Dust the work surface with flour. Flour the dough on all sides and, with a rolling pin or the heels of your palms, extend it to a thin round, about 1/8 inch thick. The dough will rise some more as it bakes.

5. With a 2-inch-diameter cookie cutter or other utensil, cut the dough into rounds. On the middle of each, place a teaspoon of filling. Fold over to form a half-moon. Dip the fork tines into flour and press to seal and decorate the edges. Place on a cookie sheet. (If you have filling left over, scramble later with a couple of eggs and enjoy.)

6. Brush the tops with a beaten egg and bake in the preheated oven for 30 minutes. The pastries should be light golden brown when you remove them from the oven. Let them cool a bit and serve. You may also serve them cold at a picnic.

For the pastry dough:

2 1/2 cups all-purpose flour

1/2 teaspoon yeast

1 teaspoon salt

1/4 cup (1/2 stick) butter

1/3 cup olive oil

1 egg, slightly beaten

1/2 cup Greek yogurt or sour cream

For the savory filling:

1 cup crumbled feta

1/2 cup grated Parmesan or other hard and aged cheese

3 tablespoons heavy cream

1 egg

2 scallions, chopped fine

1 tablespoon dill

Flour or cornstarch for dusting

1 beaten egg yolk with a drop of cold water, for brushing

45

 March 25

On this double holiday of Independence Day and Annunciation, the two great loves of the Greek Orthodox combine: love of country and love of the Virgin, called Panayía, or more familiarly Panayiá.

The words *Eikosipénte tou Martioú*, twenty-fifth of March, Independence Day, evoke the sounds of church bells and parade marches in the memory of every Greek who had an education in the country. It is a thrilling holiday in the most profoundly nationalistic sense—the day the War of Independence against the Turks was announced by a bishop, Palaión Patrón Ghermanós, in southern Greece—the date indelible, March 25, 1821.

After nearly four centuries of occupation, from the date of the fall of Byzantium engraved in every Greek brain, 1453, the Greeks began to assert their independence. The war became extremely complicated, lasting for many years, until finally southern Greece was truly liberated. Like every war, it has its undying myths, its heroes and scoundrels, its songs and poetry. What interests me here is that a way of cooking meat arose from that experience. Let me explain.

After the fall of Constantinople, which meant the fall of Byzantium, many Greeks took to the hills, mainly as brigands (*kléftes*), and much later as fighting guerrillas, to escape and to undermine the occupier Turks. If you visit Greece, especially Epirus, you will discover how easy it would be to hide in those impressive mountains and how harsh and ferocious life must have been for those who lived there. History tells us that in order not to be discovered by the Turks, the *kléftes* buried the meat so that it would cook without the telltale smell and smoke of roasting. From Epirus itself (Épeiros in Greek), legendary for its courageous women, we have *arní sti stámna*, "lamb in a clay water jug." The women would appear to be carrying water when indeed they were feeding their men.

From this hidden practice arose the recipe called *kléftiko* (see page 65) or *exohikó* (see page 154). *Kléftiko* refers to meat with vegetables enclosed in paper and cooked in a hole in the earth, or nowadays in the oven. One cooking method from the island of Crete may be still duplicated today by those who have the courage, the time, and the space. Dig a pit in the earth and light a fire that should get very, very hot. Remove the hot coals, place a whole lamb or goat, gutted but with the skin on, inside the pit, cover with earth, and pile the hot coals on top. Keep the fire going for twenty-four hours. Then unearth the animal and you are ready for a feast for many. To make *kléftiko* at home, you may choose an easier method (see page 65). But first, a word about the second half of the holiday.

The twin of this national holiday is a religious one, the day of the Annunciation, the good news brought to Mary of Nazareth by the angel Gabriel—*evangelismós* in Greek. The Greek Orthodox have a love affair with the person of Mary, whom they call Panayía, the All Holy, and Theotókos, the God Bearer. Words, of course, are very revealing. I'm afraid, however, that in this instance the national fervor overwhelms the religious one, though the two are so intertwined in the national consciousness that I am offering recipes that can apply to both.

White Bean Salad

Ghíghantes Saláta

1 pound *ghíghantes* beans

Salt and pepper

1/2 cup olive oil, plus 2 tablespoons for finish

1/4 cup lemon juice, plus
1 tablespoon for finish

5–6 scallions, white parts with
a bit of the green, sliced in
fine rounds

1/4 cup chopped flat-leaf
parsley

10 Kalamata olives, pitted

2 cucumbers, halved lengthwise and sliced

2 tomatoes, cut in four
segments and then sliced

Ghíghantes means giants. These beans from Greece are found through websites or at Greek markets. They are white, similar to large lima beans, but what is distinctive about them is that the beans hold their shape and jackets after soaking and expanding. You will need to prepare ahead.

Serves 10

1. Soak the beans in cold water overnight. You will need your largest bowl, since they double in size. If you can manage it, change the water a couple of times.

2. When you are ready to cook the beans, rinse and drain them well. Bring an 8-quart pot of water to a boil and add the beans, without salt. If you have a pressure cooker, they will cook very fast, but in a regular pot it will take about 2 hours until they soften and can be cut with a fork. Drain, place inside a large, wide bowl, and toss with salt and pepper.

3. Whisk 1/2 cup oil with 1/4 cup lemon juice, add the scallions, and pour all over the beans. Toss again to coat thoroughly.

4. Now add the parsley for both color and taste. Decorate with black olives. Cover and refrigerate.

5. Just before serving, whisk together the remaining olive oil and lemon juice. Top the bean salad with sliced cucumbers and tomatoes, pour the finishing dressing on these, and serve. I like to offer additional dressing for individual use. I keep this on hand: one part lemon juice to two parts olive oil.

Variation: These beans may also be served hot, which I do often in winter. Chop and sauté an onion, a stalk of celery, and 2 carrots in 1/4 cup olive oil. Add 1 can tomato paste diluted in 4 cups water, 1/4 cup snipped parsley, and 2–3 cups of the beans after they have soaked overnight. Cook on top of the stove for 2 hours, then pour everything into a deep casserole and bake uncovered for 1 hour at 400°F, adding liquid as needed. Serve with lemon wedges and freshly ground pepper.

Salt Cod

Bakaliáros

Bakaliáros (bacalao in Spanish), or salt cod, is very popular in Greece, as are many delicious kinds of sardines that are preserved in salt. Although cod is a cold-water fish that comes from northern seas, *bakaliáros* is still considered quite Greek because it is enjoyed both on March 25 and on Palm Sunday.

1 pound salt cod

1 cup flour

1/2 teaspoon baking powder

1 cup ice water

2 teaspoons lemon juice

1 egg (optional)

Olive oil for frying

Serves 4

1. The salted fish must be soaked for many hours—two days are recommended, though overnight will do. Place it in cold water, cover, and refrigerate, changing the water periodically, until ready to cook. Then rinse and dry well, remove skin and bones, and cut into serving pieces.

2. Make a batter, called *kourkoúti*, of the flour, baking powder, ice water, and lemon juice. Mix well to a thick consistency; you may add a beaten egg to make it richer.

3. Dip the fish portions in the *kourkoúti* to coat well, and fry in olive oil until golden. Drain on paper towels. When all the fish is cooked, serve it with garlic sauce, *skordhaliá*.

Note: This recipe is also delicious with fresh cod.

Garlic Sauce

Skordhaliá

This sauce or side dish, quite distinctly flavored with garlic, comes in two versions, one made with potatoes, the other with bread. You will need a good-sized mortar and pestle for best results (a food processor makes the potatoes a glutinous mess). The accompaniment of *skordhaliá* greatly enhances certain foods—the fish *bakaliáros* (page 50); also beets, greens, vegetable croquettes. Just make sure everyone eats some of it!

3 medium potatoes, boiled in their skins

4–5 cloves garlic, or fewer, depending on taste

1 teaspoon kosher salt

1/3 cup olive oil, plus 1 teaspoon

1/4 cup white vinegar

1/2 cup hot water (optional)

Makes 2 1/2–3 cups

1. Peel potatoes and mash with a fork.

2. Place the peeled garlic in the mortar. Add the salt and 1 teaspoon olive oil, and mash with the pestle until you have a paste. Add the mashed potatoes and keep working them in the mortar until they attain a smooth consistency.

3. Add olive oil while still working the pestle. The national tendency is to use a great deal of oil, but I start with 1/4 cup and move to 1/3, and that to me is rich enough. Experiment until you have the consistency you like.

4. Now add the vinegar, a tablespoon at a time, to taste. You may substitute lemon juice. I don't find the need to add more salt, but you may want to adjust the amount. Thin this sauce with a bit of hot water if it gets too stiff.

5. Cover very tightly (garlic has a tendency to permeate other foods in the refrigerator). The flavor will improve after a couple of hours. Serve at room temperature. When you serve beets (see page 53) with *skordhaliá*, you don't need seasoning except lemon juice, which brings out their sweetness.

Variation: In my home we preferred to use soaked bread instead of potatoes. You need bread that doesn't disintegrate when wet and that holds its volume—day-old French or Italian or, in my case, Greek. Cut all the crust off (use enough bread to result in 2 cups crustless bread). Plunge the bread into warm water, let it soak through, then squeeze the water out. Using this wet mass in place of the potatoes, proceed as above. You may thin this sauce also with hot water.

Beets with Stems and Leaves

Pantzarosaláta

Beets are so filled with fine possibilities, it is a pity that so many cooks ignore them. You can eat them hot or cold, boiled or roasted, pickled or sweet, by themselves or combined with other vegetables, and they are good for you and good to eat in every way.

Usually sold in bunches of three, they are a deep maroon red or golden brown.

3 beets with leaves and stems

1 tablespoon vinegar

1 tablespoon salt

Lemon juice

Serves 6

1. Cut off the stems and leaves of the beets without piercing the bulb. Set leaves with stems aside. Scrub the beets thoroughly under cold water.

2. Boil a 2-quart pot of water. Add the vinegar and salt, then the beets, and cover. Boil for about 1 hour. They should be soft enough to pierce with a fork. Remove them and run cold water over them. Beets are easier to peel when warm. Just rub the outer skin off, slice them across in rounds, and place them on a platter in overlapping circles.

3. Meanwhile, wash well, cut in small pieces, and boil the leaves and stems until the stems are tender. Drain and pile in the middle of the beet circles.

4. Drizzle everything with lemon juice. You can eat them just as they are, but they are really delicious with *skordhaliá* (see page 51). You can also dress them with olive oil and vinegar, snipped dill or parsley, and, if you like it, sliced raw onion.

Leeks with Rice

Prasórizo

4 tablespoons butter

2 large washed leeks, white
and light green parts only
(4–5 cups cut up; see note)

1 cup rice

1 1/2 teaspoon sea salt

1 teaspoon sugar

Pepper, to taste

1/4 cup snipped dill

4 tablespoons lemon juice

It took a long time for me to start cooking with the wonderful leek, another ancient vegetable. The supermarkets in the southern town where I lived for years did not stock leeks until I asked for them from a grocer I knew. The leek has been eaten in the Mediterranean region for a long, long time, and I always keep two or three in my vegetable bin. They look like very thick, very large scallions, but their taste is much milder. A simple dish that combines this versatile vegetable with rice, *prasórizo* is simple, delicious, and reminds one of child-hood. It is not considered fancy, but it is tasty and so easy. By the way, the name *prasórizo* comes from *práso* for leek and *rízi* for rice.

Serves 10

1. Melt butter over medium heat in a pan 10–12 inches in diameter. Cut the leeks crosswise into thin rings. Sauté in the butter, stirring often until they begin to wilt; add the rice and stir so the kernels are well coated.

2. Pour 2 cups warm water into the pan and stir well. Add sea salt, sugar, and freshly ground pepper to taste. Stir. Add another 1/2 cup water.

3. Cover and simmer. Watch to make sure the rice doesn't burn; add water as needed until the rice is tender.

4. Add dill and lemon juice, and serve hot or cold as a side dish.

Note: To prep leeks for cooking, cut off the very end (remaining root) and the dark green leaves. Discard leaves or save for stock. You want to work with the white or light green, tightly pressed multiple layers. Cut this long and thick stalk vertically and, separating the layers with your fingers, run cold water through them until all the sand is washed out. Now you are ready to use them in a variety of ways.

Spinach with Rice

Spanakórizo

When thinking of rice cooked with vegetables, one must not forget *spanakórizo*. A recipe I closely associate with childhood memories, it is truly a lovely dish—earthy yet delicate.

1 clove garlic, chopped fine

3 scallions, finely sliced

1/4 cup olive oil

1/2 cup rice

1 pound baby spinach

1/4 cup snipped dill

1 teaspoon salt

1 teaspoon pepper

Juice of 1 lemon

Lemon slices for serving

Serves 6

1. Sauté the garlic and scallions in the olive oil until just translucent; add the rice and stir to coat. Add 1 cup water and then the spinach. Cover the pan and allow the spinach to wilt for about 10 minutes. Now add the dill, salt, and pepper. Stir well, add another cup of water, and cover tightly, setting the heat to simmer.

2. Check in about 30 minutes to see if the rice is done; if not, add 1/2 cup water and continue simmering until water is absorbed and rice is cooked.

3. Pour the lemon juice over the dish and stir gently. Remove from heat, remove pan cover, place a clean tea towel over the dish, and cover with the lid. Let rest for 10 minutes.

4. Taste and adjust lemon and salt. Serve in a bowl with slices of lemon; you may offer feta with it, but the taste is complete in itself.

Cookie Twists

Koulourákia

This is a recipe I have used and enjoyed for decades. Children and grandchildren and all their friends quickly learned to pronounce this four-syllable word with ease.

Makes 40 cookies

1. In a mixer or by hand whip the oil with the sugar until very light and frothy, then add the 4 eggs one at a time, whipping well after each addition. Mix baker's ammonia or baking powder with flour. Add 4 cups flour, 1 cup at a time, while whipping at low speed. Add the extracts (I vary these flavors just for interest).

2. Move the dough to a work surface and add flour, a little at a time, until you can handle the dough, which must not feel dry. At this stage you may cover and refrigerate, or start shaping the *koulourákia*.

3. Preheat the oven to 360°F.

4. Taking a pinch of dough, roll it into a slender rope. Form one or more ropes into braids, figure eights, or all kinds of imaginative designs. When the children are present, let them make their own designs. They love it. Place the finished shapes on baking sheets lined with parchment paper. Then brush all of the cookies with a wash of 2 beaten egg yolks whipped with 2 drops of cold water.

5. Bake until golden, about 20 minutes. In a covered container, *koulourákia* last a very long time, and their flavor only improves. Perfect for coffee.

1 cup corn oil or organic shortening

1 1/2 cups sugar (or 2 cups if you want the cookies sweeter)

4 large eggs

3/4 teaspoon baker's ammonia (see note) or 1/2 teaspoon baking powder

4–6 cups flour, plus more for dusting

1 teaspoon vanilla extract or almond extract

1 teaspoon orange extract or lemon extract

2 egg yolks, for the finish

Note: Baker's ammonia (ammonium bicarbonate) has nothing to do with ammonia for cleaning; this powder is found in specialty shops or on websites.

Sesame Cookies

Sousamákia

2 1/4 cups all-purpose flour

1 1/2 sticks butter, at room temperature

2/3 cup sugar

1 egg, separated

1 cup sesame seeds

This delicious and easy recipe is from my sister-in-law, Soula.

Makes 30 cookies

1. Preheat oven to 360°F.

2. Put the flour, butter, sugar, and the yolk of the egg in a food processor and pulse until you have a very coarse meal. Transfer into a large bowl and, working with your hands, form the dough.

3. Pinch a bit at a time and roll into finger-size cylinders.

4. In a small bowl beat the egg white with a drop of water. Spread the sesame on a plate. Take each cookie, dip it in the egg white, and then roll in the sesame. Place on baking sheets lined with parchment paper.

5. Bake for about 30 minutes, or until rosy brown. The cookies will be soft when they come out of the oven, so be careful they don't break when you move them.

6. Let them cool on the paper. The exterior will harden as they cool, but the interior remains soft. In a tightly closed tin they will keep for quite a few days.

COOKIES

Greeks love cookies with our coffee or tea. They are called *voutímata* because they are for *dipping* in coffee, a perfectly acceptable method of eating them. Most cookies are also called *koulourákia* because their basic shape is a *kouloúra*, literally "coil," a slender rope of dough that has been wound into various rounded shapes. There are many kinds of *koulourákia*, and they are all lovely to look at and a pleasure to eat.

A Menu for March 25

White Bean Salad (*Ghíghantes Saláta*) 48

Salt Cod (*Bakaliáros*) 50

Beets with Stems and Leaves (*Pantzarosaláta*) 53

Garlic Sauce (*Skordhaliá*) 51

Fresh fruit

Cookie Twists (*Koulourákia*) 57

A Menu for a Picnic

Crusty bread or pita triangles, raw vegetables, and Greek Caviar
(*Taramosaláta*) 34

Individual Savory Pastries (*Bourekákia*) 45

Grape Leaves with Rice Filling (*Dolmadhákia*)
with lemon wedges 39

Meatballs (*Keftedhákia*) with mustard 43

Stuffed Eggs with Ouzo Flavor (*Methysména Avgá*) 35

Cookie Twists (*Koulourákia*) 57

Cabbage Salad

Lahanosaláta

1 small white cabbage

1/2 small red cabbage

Kosher salt

1 large carrot, peeled

2 tablespoons olive oil

2 tablespoons vinegar

Pinch of sugar

1 tablespoon snipped basil
 leaves

The main dishes in this chapter are filling, so you need a salad with a vinegary taste. This recipe fits the bill.

Serves 8

1. Two or three hours before the meal, cut the white and red cabbage into very slender strips, 4 cups altogether. Place in a colander with a platter underneath and sprinkle generously with salt, so the water will be drawn and drained. When ready to assemble the salad, taste cabbage for saltiness. If too salty, rinse and dry in towels.

2. Place cabbage in a bowl. Add the carrot, shaved into ribbons with a potato peeler.

3. For the dressing, combine the oil, vinegar, sugar, and basil in a jar with a tight lid. Shake well and pour over the salad. Toss and serve.

Yogurt and Cucumber Dip

Tzatzíki

2 small "pickling" cucumbers
(see note)

1 cup Greek yogurt (see note)

2 cloves garlic, or to taste

Pinch of salt

2 tablespoons plus 1 teaspoon
olive oil

1 tablespoon distilled vinegar
or lemon juice

Fresh dill for topping
(optional)

This is a perennial favorite. All the Americans who have visited Greece with me, including my grandchildren, insisted on starting meals with this appetizer. It is one of the most refreshing and cooling appetizers you will find.

Serves 12

1. Cut the cucumber in very small pieces. (If you are using a large cucumber, scrape the seeds out.) In a bowl combine the cucumber and yogurt. Mash the garlic in a mortar together with the salt and 1 teaspoon oil. Mix this into the yogurt and cucumber. Stir in the remaining 2 tablespoons oil and then the vinegar. Now taste. You may need to adjust it with a bit more vinegar or salt.

2. The flavor improves when you cover the *tzatzíki* tightly and refrigerate for several hours. I like to sprinkle with fresh dill before serving.

Note: The cucumbers that are best for *tzatzíki* are called "pickling" cucumbers, and they have undeveloped seeds. For the yogurt in this recipe, I find the plain Greek Gods variety excellent.

Meat Pie with Leeks

Kreatoprasópita

A note about the Greek recipe title: The Greek language combines two or three words easily to make another, here *kreas* (meat) plus *praso* (leek) and *pita* (pie). The word *pita*, plural *pites* (circa seventh century), was Byzantine Greek for "pie" (see *hortópita*, page 86) before it was applied to pocket bread by Arabs.

I make this pie in a deep, round metal pan, 14.5 inches in diameter and 3 inches deep. (Two-inch-deep cake pans are available and easier to use.) Mine is a pan often used in Greek cooking, and Greek markets sell them. In fact, I created this dish after I bought a round pan in a Greek grocery in New York. This recipe serves as many as twelve people, so it's good for a dinner party; leftovers may be frozen. *Kreatoprasópita* is a perfect dish to cook on a rainy, damp day. It seems to warm the kitchen up with good smells and the mouth with good taste.

Makes 12 to 15 generous wedges

1. Prep the leeks (see Leeks with Rice, page 54) and slice them crosswise. Blanch in boiling water until translucent. Drain, reserving the water, and set aside.

2. Brown the meat in the butter. Stir in the tomato paste diluted in 1 cup warm water, then the wine. Add the leeks, the parsley and spices, and salt and pepper to taste. Let the meat sauce simmer uncovered while you prepare the crust. You may add water left from blanching the leeks, as needed.

3. Place the flour in a bowl and stir in the yeast and salt. Add the olive oil and enough water to bring the flour together in a ball. Knead for 5 minutes, then cover and let it rest for at least half an hour while the sauce simmers.

4. Check the meat sauce to make sure it's not watery; if it is, raise the heat and boil off the excess liquid. Turn the heat off and let the sauce cool completely.

5. About 1 1/4 hours before serving, preheat the oven to 375°F.

6. Divide the dough into two segments, one larger than the other. Roll the larger one 3 inches wider than the pan's diameter and place it in the well-oiled pan, letting the dough come up and over

For the meat filling:

3 leeks

2 pounds ground beef, bison, or lamb (or any combination)

3 tablespoons butter

1 7-ounce can tomato paste

1/2 cup dry red wine

1/2 cup snipped parsley

1 teaspoon ground cumin

1/2 teaspoon cinnamon

Pinch of nutmeg (optional)

Salt and pepper, to taste

For the pastry crust:

3 1/2 cups flour

1/2 teaspoon yeast

1 tablespoon salt

1/4 cup olive oil

1/2 cup warm water (or more as needed)

8 ounces crumbled feta

1/4 cup grated Parmesan (optional)

1 tablespoon oregano

the sides of the pan. Oil the dough generously. Place the cooled filling inside the bottom crust. Cover it with cheese, and sprinkle with oregano. Roll out the remaining dough to the size of the pan's diameter and place on top. Pinch the edges and roll the two crusts together in a decorative rim, like rolling a scroll. Brush generously with olive oil and cut slits on the surface.

7. Bake for 1 hour; make sure the top is crusty and rosy. With *pita* in a very large round pan, the Greeks cut a circle in the middle, about 4 inches in diameter, then radiate the wedges from the edge of this circle to the edge of the pan.

Lamb Baked in Paper
Kléftiko

Kléftiko is a term that derives from our history of resistance. Many Greeks took refuge in the wild mountains of the mainland after the fall of Constantinople. There they lived as brigands (*kléftes*) and later, especially during the War for Independence, as guerrillas. In order not to be detected by the enemy when they roasted meat—the smoke and aroma are such traitors of the cooks' presence—they would wrap the meat and bury it to cook it; hence *kléftiko*, the meat of the guerrillas.

Serves 6

1. Preheat oven to 360°F.

2. Prepare the wrapping for the *kleftiko* by cutting two 30-inch lengths of twine and crisscrossing them on the bottom of a baking pan. Place the two sheets of parchment paper over them, crisscrossing the paper so it covers the pan bottom with enough paper left over to enclose the ingredients. Score slits in the meat and stuff with garlic cloves. Rub well with oregano and rosemary, salt and pepper, and place in the parchment-lined pan. Add the potatoes, celery, and carrots, cut into serving pieces. Drizzle with olive oil. Wrap well in the parchment paper so that everything is enclosed, then tie with twine. (You may need another parchment sheet laid on top and tied underneath.)

3. Place the pan with the parchment package in the preheated oven for 2 hours for rare, 2 1/2 hours for medium. Remove from the oven and place the roasting pan with the paper package on the counter; wait half an hour before opening and slicing.

Variation: Another version of this very simple, very good dish is to cook the lamb with herbs but without vegetables in parchment and serve with orzo or pilaf. If you have a large clay pot with lid, choose that instead of the paper.

Parchment paper cut in two 15- x 25-inch lengths

1 5-pound leg of lamb

5 garlic cloves, peeled

1 tablespoon oregano

1 tablespoon rosemary

Sea salt and pepper

3 potatoes, peeled and quartered

2 celery stalks

2 carrots, peeled

1/4 cup olive oil

Shredded Phyllo Pastry

Kadaífi

1 pound *kadaífi* dough

2 sticks unsalted butter

1 1/2 cups finely chopped
walnuts or almonds

2 teaspoons cinnamon

1 teaspoon cloves

1/3 cup sugar

For the syrup (see note):

2 cups sugar

2 1/2 cups water

3 whole cloves

1 teaspoon lemon juice

Kadaífi pastry is a delicious dessert when prepared with excellent ingredients. Baklava is almost foolproof, but this is a bit more difficult; I greatly prefer it when it is just right. I have found *kadaífi* dough in some supermarkets frozen like phyllo; it can also be ordered online. The uncooked pastry looks like shredded wheat cereal, but it is actually dough that has been finely shredded.

Serves 20

1. Preheat oven to 350°F.

2. When the *kadaífi* thaws, pull it apart with your fingers—a bit like fluffing wool—to separate and loosen the strands of dough. Make sure this is done, because the strands will be stuck together even when thawed. Melt the butter, then pour it on top of and through the *kadaífi* strands. Spread half of the well-buttered dough inside a 12 x 9 x 2-inch metal pan. (At this stage, you may add more melted butter if you wish.)

3. Mix the nuts with the spices and sugar. Spread this mixture over the buttered dough. Now spread the remainder of the dough over the filling. Sprinkle drops of cold water on the top and bake in the preheated oven for 35 minutes; the *kadaífi* will become rosy in color and will shrink from the sides of the pan when it is done.

4. While it is baking, prepare the syrup: Boil together all ingredients; let the syrup reach 230°F. Remove and cool to about 120°F.

5. When you bring out the hot pastry, pour half of the cooled syrup over it, cover the pan with aluminum foil, and let it rest for 10 minutes. Uncover, pour the rest of the syrup over the pastry, cover again with the foil, and let it steam; this steaming is very important. After a couple of hours pass, uncover it and feel the top layer of the pastry. If it still feels dry, upend the whole thing into a larger pan so that the syrup from the bottom layer penetrates the top layer of the dessert.

6. Ideally, try to make this dish a day ahead and uncover it the next. Cut in squares with a spatula and serve. Some serve it with whipped cream, but I prefer it with just fruit. *Kadaífi* keeps for quite a while when tightly covered in a sealed container. It may also be frozen.

❧ The Day of Ascension ❧
and Sweet Celebrations from Asia Minor

Unless you belong to a community of highly observant Christians, you rarely ever hear of Ascension Day in America. Roman Catholics and Anglicans observe it, since it is one of the major feasts of the church, commemorating the end of Jesus's earthly presence. But the Orthodox have many customs and traditions that reveal how important this fortieth day from Resurrection, a Thursday, is in the life of the country. It's a bank holiday, and traditionally the day when people go for their first swim in the sea before summer arrives. The citizens of the island of Samos bring this seawater back home to sprinkle all over the house, saying that as Christ was taken up (disappeared), so let all bad words and meanness and illness disappear, especially the evil eye. Greek Orthodox, with few exceptions, are great believers in the evil eye and do everything in their power to avert it—which proves again that the ancient fears are not far from the collective subconscious. The Samians keep this seawater of Ascension Day throughout the year to use on hurts or whenever the evil eye is suspected of having entered the home.

On Ascension Day shepherds do not keep any of the milk or cheese produced but give it away. This is good for them and for their animals, they believe (perhaps an ancient remnant of the first time shepherds heard the commandments of the gospel, to care for the least of God's people?). On this day they feed salt to their sheep and goats, believing this aids their productivity. In the middle of the day, for the unique pastoral people called Sarakatsans—who consider this their own holiday—comes the time of eating, drinking, and dancing that is led by the oldest in the community.

And in the southernmost part of the mainland, Koróni, the people stay up all night to watch the skies where Jesus ascended. It is said that the pure in heart see a light that ascends into the heavens. A biblical echo: "Blessed are the pure in heart, for they shall see God."

Since Ascension Day comes after Easter, meat is allowed. I give here appropriate meat recipes for the main meal of the day, in addition to starters, sides, and desserts, our heritage in sweet celebrations from Asia Minor Greeks.

Most of the desserts with unusual custards and a syrupy finish come from the Greeks who arrived as refugees to the mainland from Asia Minor, where a splendid

Greek civilization had flourished from classical times, through the Turkish occupation, until the disaster of 1922. The catastrophe of '22 is well known to every child who studies Greek history and to every adult who is familiar with our literature. It is a poignant, heartbreaking story of loss. One and a half million displaced persons from Asia Minor had to be assimilated into the population of a country that was very poor at that time. (For the tragedy and the memories and the ache, I suggest you read poets like George Seféris, novels like *The Schoolmistress with the Golden Eyes* by Strátis Myrivílis, and even *Middlesex*, written by a Greek American, Jeffrey Eugenides.) As the decades passed, the rest of Greece recognized the wealth of culture her strange new children had brought to the motherland. My brother is married to a descendant of these Micrasiótes, people of Asia Minor, and he praises her people with a passionate appreciation for their heritage, their cooking, and their hospitality. They preserve their memories and their customs and they share with the rest of us their delectable recipes. They speak Turkish and Greek and for the most part have retained the Turkish names of their recipes. It is difficult to know who created these recipes—the Greeks who were there for centuries, or the Turks who, compared to the millennia of Greek existence on the lands bordering the Aegean to the east, are relative newcomers. The fact remains that the recipes are delicious, and I will leave it at that.

I will focus here only on two recipes that are most certainly associated with Asia Minor Greeks. The emphasis on milk shows us how pastoral many Greek people have been for centuries; in fact the unique Sarakatsans, a shepherd culture hidden from the rest of Greece for decades, were able to retain strong customs that were utterly dependent on the grazing season. Every sweet recipe has a unique variation in each major section of the land. One of them is most unusual; during a recent visit reminiscing with my sister, she asked, "Do you remember the Boughatsa shops in Thessaloniki that served Taouk Yioukchou?" Just the name stunned me and brought back the image of something white and creamy but with the consistency of Jell-O, and from the depths of memory a taste came back, delectable and never since encountered. "I think they made it out of chicken breast," she said. When I found the recipe I was excited, but the result still did not satisfy me—the chicken is not supposed to be discernible, but no matter how hard I tried, there was still the texture of chicken in the custard. So I offer a couple of substitutes, Greek Crème Brûlée (page 71) and Thin Pie (page 72).

Custard from Asia Minor (the Greek Crème Brûlée)

Kazán Dipí

The recipe is known by its Turkish name, *kazán dipí*, which means the bottom of the pot. It comes from the Asia Minor club of the city of Xánthi, in the northeastern part of Greece. When I was growing up, Xánthi was considered an outpost, poor and remote. Now it's a thriving city, with beautiful architecture and the nightlife of the young, which has become so characteristic of modern Greek cities. The Asia Minor Greeks with their pride of heritage have done much to promote and restore their town. This area was part of Alexander's ancient Macedonia and of Thrace. Language and customs have bound the people into a homogenous Greek populace. The feel, looks, and taste of this custard were buried somewhere deep within me where memories of childhood hold smells and tastes thought forgotten.

2 tablespoons melted butter

1 cup plus 2–3 tablespoons sugar

2 tablespoons plain cornmeal

1 cup all-purpose flour

5 cups whole milk, chilled

1 generous teaspoon vanilla or almond extract

Cinnamon (optional)

Serves 12

1. Preheat the oven to 350°F.

2. Spread the melted butter on the bottom of a 12 x 9 x 2-inch non-stick pan. Sprinkle 2–3 tablespoons sugar over it and place in the preheated oven until the sugar begins to turn a caramel color and melt. Now remove the pan from the oven.

3. Mix the cornmeal and flour together, then whisk into the chilled milk until no lumps remain. Pour into a 3-quart pot. Over low to medium flame, stir gently until the mixture begins to thicken, about 10 minutes.

4. Now add the remaining 1 cup of sugar and stir 1 minute. Remove from heat and add the extract; stir to combine. Pour into the prepared sugared pan, return to the oven, and bake for 15–20 minutes. The custard will not be totally set.

5. Remove the pan from the oven and place inside a larger pan that contains cold water. As the custard cools, it will set. Add a few pieces of ice to the water bath to keep it cold. The custard will continue to set after you remove it from the cold bath and upend it on a serving platter.

6. Sprinkle with cinnamon, and enjoy.

Thin Pie

Ahamnópita

1 cup sugar

1 stick unsalted butter

4 cups milk

4 ounces unbleached flour

4 eggs

1 teaspoon vanilla extract

Another version of *kazán dipí* (page 71), this one traditional just for the Day of Ascension, is a milk pie called *ahamnópita*, which means a "thin" or "liquid" pie.

Serves 10

1. Preheat convection oven to 325°F, conventional to 300°F.

2. In a 2-quart pot melt the sugar and butter together. In a 2-quart bowl pour the milk and beat in the flour so there are no lumps. Add the flour-milk mixture to the melted sugar and butter and stir; the mixture will be hot but not boiling. Now in a cold bowl beat the eggs together with the vanilla. Stir a scoop of the warm milk mixture into the eggs to season them for the heat; repeat several times, then add this to the warm milk mixture. Stir well. Pour the liquid into a 12 x 9 x 2-inch nonstick metal baking pan.

3. Carefully place the pan in the oven. The batter will be very thin and watery, but will set in the oven. The old-timers said that it needed to be stirred several times while baking, but I have not found this necessary. Remove when set, about 45 minutes.

4. Serve warm with cinnamon, or perhaps instead of pancakes for breakfast.

A Sample Menu for Ascension Day

Raw vegetables with Yogurt and Cucumber Dip
(*Tzatzíki*) 62

Meat Pie with Leeks (*Kreatoprasópita*) 63
or Lamb Baked in Paper (*Kléftiko*) 65

Seasonal fruit

In the evening, with coffee,

Shredded Phyllo Pastry (*Kadaífi*) 66
or Custard from Asia Minor (*Kazán Dipí*) 71

Stuffed Zucchini Flowers I
(*Korfádhes Ghemistés*)

Stuffed Zucchini Flowers II
(*Korfádhes Ghemistés*)

Stuffed Zucchini with Meat Sauce
(*Kolokýthia Ghemistá*)

The Famous Greek Salad
(*Horiátiki Saláta*)

Greens in a Pie
(*Hortópita*)

Chard and Other Greens with Croutons
(*Hórta me Psomákia*)

Eggplant with Feta
(*Melitzánes me Feta*)

Stuffed Eggplant
(*Moussaká Papoutsákia*)

Sweet Cheese Pies from Crete
(*Kaltsoúnia Krítis*)

Sweet Cheese Pie in Phyllo
(*Glykiá Tyrópita*)

Chapter 3

THE PENTECOST SEASON OPENS: SPRING

*P*entecost falls on the fiftieth day counting from Easter Sunday, hence the number *pente* for five in the word. In Christian theology and tradition, this is the day when God sent the Holy Spirit to the disciples bereft of Jesus's earthly presence, a day when many languages were spoken and all were understood. This quality of that significant day is evident today in the many languages that are spoken around thousands of tables in many Mediterranean countries and restaurants, languages that are understood enough for people to enjoy meals together.

Pentecost in the religious sense, especially in Western theology, is the birthday of the church, but it is a comforting day as well, because in the Greek the Holy Spirit is also called Parakletés, Paraclete, the Advocate, one who intercedes for us. In the Orthodox Church tradition, advocacy is tremendously important when the faithful pray to the Virgin Mary and to saints to intercede for them. (Pentecost is not considered "the birthday of the church" by the Orthodox because they believe that the church exists from the time of Creation. It is important to note that tradition holds the utmost importance in the Orthodox understanding of the church and its theology. The season following Pentecost is the longest of the church year, extending all the way to Advent. The names for the seasons are not part of the Orthodox lexicon, but the worldwide Christian community recognizes them as such, so I am using them for this book.) The earliest part of the Pentecost season falls in late spring; it encompasses all of summer and fall, a rich time of vegetables, fruits, and harvest.

Springtime of Myths and Flowers

When May the first, Protomayiá, arrives in Greece, it is easy to believe that little has changed from ancient times in the awareness of new life on earth. In times before recording and memory, the goddess Démetra (Demeter) was revered in mysteries (forms of worship) that have remained mysterious, unknown to us after all the centuries. In the southern city of Eleusis, in the lovely, light-filled small museum dedicated to the goddess, one feels a different spirit in the sculpted presence of this female deity so ingrained into the psyche of her worshipers. The myth is well known, and my grandchildren early on understood its connection to the seasons.

Démetra had a daughter, Persephónê (and since this was my mother's name, we paid attention), a lovely girl who, while playing in the blooming fields, was abducted by the god of the underworld, Hades, to become his wife. All blooms and laughter left the earth and people were dying from Démetra's grief. Long negotiations among the Olympians finally reached a compromise: Démetra could have her daughter during spring and summer, and Hades could have his wife during fall and winter. Thus the seasons were understood by our ancestors.

Blossoms start in Greece in late winter, with the astounding beauty of the flowering almond tree in February, its praises sung with lyrical love by our poets. By May 1 the earth is covered with the red of the poppies and the yellow-white of the chamomile. Both were well known to the ancients for their medicinal properties. And they were not ignorant of the danger of the poppy, called *paparoúna* in the Greek, the one who sheds her leaves quickly. The twin sons of Nyx (Night), associated with *paparoúnes*, were called Hypnos (Sleep) and Thánatos (Death). The light use of the *paparoúna* brought sleepiness; the heavy use, death. Démetra's temple and statue were festooned with *paparoúnes*.

Chamomile, covering the earth like a blanket, releases its unique aroma when stepped upon and featured greatly in our childhood, when it was drunk to heal upset tummies and sore throats. Thousands of other wildflowers also bloom and shed their aromas and petals at this time. The Greeks from ancient times have decorated their doors with these flowers in the form of wreaths, and in the cities they hang them from the balconies.

Greeks from Asia Minor placed a head of garlic among the flowers to avert the evil eye, a thistle (thorn) to discourage the enemy, and a wheat stalk to bring in a good harvest.

On the island of Kefaloniá, in the Ionian Sea, according to the ancient holiday of Anthesphoria, which was the festival of flowers, the workers celebrated together with business owners on this first day in May. I wonder if this is the reason that, in many other countries as well as in Greece, May Day is still associated with the rights of workers.

Almost every day in May seems to have its own customs, but modern life has done away with many of them. What seems evident from the retelling of these customs, however, is that May is depicted as a feminine month, yet, strangely, weddings were avoided in this month, a Roman prejudice that left its imprint on conquered cultures and lingers into modern times. The Greeks, notoriously superstitious, consider marriages in the month of May to be plagued with bad luck, probably because in Roman times the month of May contained the festival of Lemuria, associated with the remembrance of the dead. Marriages may be avoided, but picnics with lots of good food predominate on this day.

GREEK CUISINE AND FLOWERS

Greek cuisine has an interesting connection to flowers. The most beloved comes from the aromatic red rose which Greeks delight in preserving. Nothing brings me so intensely to my childhood days as the aroma of rose petals simmering in sugar water or found in a jar. Though I rarely eat the preserves, I keep them for their color and the poignancy of that aroma that fills me with memories of my grandmother. The Greek cuisine also makes good use of rosewater, not as much as in the Middle East but sufficiently for you to encounter it in these pages.

Every fruit that grows in Greece is preserved, the most favored being the apricot and the sour cherry. But Greeks also preserve baby eggplant, fresh tiny walnuts, small tomatoes, and dates. This is an ancient practice. When I was a child it was customary to offer the following to a guest, soon after she arrived and took a seat: On a silver tray we placed a crystal glass with cold water and a small crystal plate holding a silver spoon filled with the spoon sweet of the day—cherries, bitter orange, apricot. It was my duty to offer this to the guest, who ate the sweet, then lifted the glass to offer a wish to the household before drinking it.

Stuffed Zucchini Flowers I

Korfádhes Ghemistés

6 zucchini blossoms, preferably with zucchini still attached

1 cup scallions, sliced in thin rounds

1/4 cup olive oil

1/2 cup rice

2 tomatoes, peeled and chopped, about 1 cup

1 cup white wine

3 tablespoons snipped mint leaves

1/4 cup snipped dill

1/4 cup snipped parsley

Salt and pepper, to taste

Juice of 1/2 lemon

One summer we were at my sister Niki's restored, exquisite house dating from two centuries back on the peninsula of Pelion, famous as the domain of the centaurs and of unparalleled green beauty. While looking at a local person's garden, she said, "You know, they stuff the flower of the zucchini here," and she showed me the delicate tulip-like yellow-gold flower while sharing this recipe. If you have friends who grow their own zucchini, ask them to let you have some with the flowers still on. In Greece, the blossoms are sold in the markets. If you like this recipe, you may want to ask your farmers' market to save them for you.

Serves 6

1. You will need a straight-sided container like a vase. Keep the blossoms attached to the vegetables and soak the 6 zucchini in cold water without wetting the flowers. Leave overnight or for several hours. (If your blossoms come without zucchini, use as soon as possible.)

2. Sauté scallions in 1/4 cup olive oil, add the rice, stir, add the tomatoes and wine, and simmer until rice has absorbed the liquids. It will be al dente.

3. Throughout the cooking process, keep checking to make sure rice doesn't dry out. Add water as needed. At the end add the herbs and salt and pepper and let cool.

4. Now very carefully, for they are fragile, remove each flower from the vegetable by cutting through the top of the zucchini. Gently stuff with the rice mixture, and bring the top together to close. Lay the flowers on their side in a well-oiled saucepan in which the flowers will lie snugly.

5. Very carefully, putting the lip of your cup at the edge of the pan, pour in enough water to almost cover the flowers, then add the lemon juice. Put an inverted plate on top of the flowers to keep them together. Bring the water to a boil, cover the pan, and reduce to a simmer. It will take about 15 minutes for the blossoms to become tender and the rice fully cooked. Serve immediately.

Stuffed Zucchini Flowers II

Korfádhes Ghemistés

This superb recipe for stuffed zucchini flowers comes from my sister Niki, who ate something similar on the island of Crete and recreated it.

Prepare zucchini blossoms as on page 78. Mix feta, egg, dill, and bread crumbs. Fill zucchini blossoms, gently dust with flour, and fry in olive oil until they turn a rosy color, about 10 minutes.

6 zucchini blossoms

1 cup crumbled feta

1 egg, lightly beaten

1/2 cup snipped dill

1/4 cup bread crumbs

Flour for dusting

1/4 cup olive oil

Stuffed Zucchini with Meat Sauce

Kolokýthia Ghemistá

6 medium-size zucchini
(3 pounds total)

1 pound ground meat or
poultry of your choice

2 tablespoons butter

1 whole onion, chopped

2–3 tomatoes, peeled and
chopped, the juice saved, or
1 14-ounce can tomatoes

1 tablespoon dried thyme

1/2 cup snipped parsley

2–3 mint or basil leaves,
snipped

Salt and pepper

2 additional tomatoes for
topping

4 ounces feta

1 cup bread crumbs

2 tablespoons melted butter,
for finish

This is a light version of the traditional moussaka casseroles. You can eat it in the summer and enjoy the freshness.

Serves 6

1. Preheat oven to 350°F.

2. Halve the zucchini lengthwise, scoop out the pulp, and save it. (When zucchini are young and small, the seeds have not developed, and that is the kind I prefer.) Blanch the halves in boiling water and, very carefully, with slotted spatulas, remove and place them snugly side by side in a 14 x 11 x 3-inch glass or CorningWare baking dish.

3. Brown the meat in the butter together with the onion. Add the tomato pulp, reserved zucchini pulp, thyme, parsley, and mint. Season with salt and pepper and let the sauce simmer until the liquid from the meat and tomatoes is absorbed.

4. Stuff the meat mixture into the zucchini halves, heaping them full. Cover with slices of fresh tomato. On top of the tomato you may place thin slices of feta and finish by sprinkling with bread crumbs. Drizzle melted butter on top and bake in preheated oven for 45 minutes.

HERBS AND GREENS (HÓRTA) IN GREEK LIFE AND COOKING

In a dry climate the smell of herbs and trees in the countryside is extremely pronounced. The aroma of herbs is a tangible presence of Greece for me. When I was a young sixteen-year-old student in the United States, required by my major to practice piano and voice, I would hide in the practice room and sing of mountain thyme in Greek folk songs, and weep: "You will return to smell the thyme again." The superb writer Patrick Leigh Fermor, author of *Roumeli: Travels in Northern Greece*, digresses to his memories of World War II in Crete, where he fought the Germans alongside the heroic Cretans of the mountains, with side expeditions to the desert of North Africa. He writes: "The smell of many herbs filled the air. (A fragrance so powerful that it surrounds the island with a halo of sweet smells several miles in radius; it told us when we were stealthily approaching Crete by sea on moonless nights from the stinking desert, and long before we could descry the great silhouette, that we were getting near.)" Ah, yes. The smell of herbs does, indeed, permeate the air: Thyme covers the Greek mountains, but has made the honey from Mount Hymettus in Attica especially famous. The anise of Lesbos fills the air and gives ouzo its distinctive flavor and aroma. And every household in Greece has a pot of basil growing on the windowsill or balcony; shaped like a round ball, it blesses with its aroma when touched by a passing hand. *Vasilikó*—it means "royal" in its Greek name—is featured in many of our folk songs. It is grown for good luck, the bush variety with the very small leaves, but mostly in pots on the balconies of the cities.

And as you probably have already seen in this book, parsley is indispensible to the Greek cook. We use the flavorful flat-leaf variety exclusively, bought fresh every day from the neighborhood grocer. In Hellenistic and Roman times, parsley was used for the athletes' wreaths, as testified by St. Paul.

The dill weed, *ánithos*, is a greatly loved addition to cooking vegetables. *Márathon*, fennel, is also used, not as frequently as dill, but it has made both an Attic location and the marathon run world famous; the wild variety is the more popular. Laurel or bay leaves are extensively used in winter stews; called *dáphne* in Greek, laurel has the distinction of having been the herb for the Olympian victors' wreaths. Exquisite wreaths made of hammered gold in the shape of laurel leaves have been found in ancient burial places.

Rosemary and sage are also used, as they are in the pages here. One must not forget that lettuce and chicory are herbs, much beloved and extensively used in Greek cooking. And scented geraniums add to those marvelous preserved fruits. But when it comes to herbs, oregano and thyme must be the kings in Greece. There is no dish containing meat that is not flavored by these remarkable herbs in their dried form.

The hills of Greece with their wild greens that include chicory, lettuce, chard, endive, and spinach, all kinds of thistles, roots like beets, and wild artichokes and asparagus saved many lives during the starvation year 1941, imposed on the populace by both enemy and weather. There are at least twenty-eight edible wild greens, called *hórta* (grasses) by the Greeks. They are now collected, sold, and eaten for their known vitamins and other nutritional benefits and for the pleasure they give when eaten as salad, vegetable, and, above all, as *pita* (pie) fillings. As people learn more about nutrition and ecology, they recognize that our ancestors knew a great deal also about what is good for us.

The Famous Greek Salad

Horiátiki Saláta

The *horiátiki*, peasant salad in Greece, is called a "Greek salad" here, and it should be served only when there are ripe, wonderfully tasty tomatoes available. In other words, this is truly a summer salad.

Serves 6

1. Choose an oval platter, about 12 x 9 inches or larger. Slice the tomatoes in semicircles and arrange them in overlapping rows around the platter's rim. Peel the cucumbers, slice in rounds, and arrange them parallel to the tomatoes. Slice the pepper in rings and arrange in the middle of the platter. Place a couple of slices of feta in the middle of the platter with the green pepper. Add a few pepperoncini or Salonika peppers and Kalamata olives; leave them whole and place them with the feta. Add the anchovies and capers in the middle also. Slice the red onion in rings and disperse over the salad. On top of everything, sprinkle the parsley and the basil or fresh mint, the dried oregano, and the salt, and then grind black pepper over the whole platter.

2. Whip the olive oil with the wine vinegar and pour over the salad.

Note: If at all possible choose a thin-skinned, small pepper that still smells like a pepper. The very large, thick-skinned peppers that stuff well are not right for this salad.

4 tomatoes

6 small cucumbers

1 small green pepper (see note)

4 ounces imported best-quality feta

4 pepperoncini (preferably Krinos brand)

4 oil-packed anchovies, drained

1 dozen pitted Kalamata olives

1 tablespoon capers, rinsed

1 red onion

3 tablespoons snipped flat-leaf parsley

2 leaves basil or fresh mint, shredded

1 tablespoon oregano

1 teaspoon salt

Freshly ground black pepper, to taste

4 tablespoons olive oil, or more to taste

2 tablespoons good wine vinegar, or more to taste

Greens in a Pie

Hortópita

For the crust:

2 cups unbleached all-purpose flour, plus more for kneading

1/2 cup whole wheat flour

1 tablespoon salt

2 teaspoons baking powder

1/2 cup beer mixed with 1/2 cup warm water (approximate)

4 tablespoons olive oil, plus more for brushing

Cornstarch, for rolling out the dough

I was just becoming interested in cooking and experimenting in the kitchen when I went to Pelion one unforgettable season, the children still young. Up to then, like every Greek, I was familiar with spanakopita and baked it often. On a visit to a taverna in Portaria's village square, the wife of the taverna owner offered us *hortópita*, a greens-filled *pita* (pie). More recently I encountered it on the island of Naxos, a large island with lovely beaches and an almost medieval interior, fabled from the myth of Theseus and Ariadne, who was claimed there by the god Dionysos. I learned then that the hills, rich in wild greens, offer us many more choices than spinach for *pita* fillings.

Traditionally, the *pita* was cooked in a round aluminum pan with a copper bottom and 2-inch-high sides. The dough was made, cut, and sold by the kilo in a specialty shop near our apartment, and as a child I would go with an order from my mother. The baker would wrap the requested weight cylindrically in white paper, and I would carry it back home to be assembled into a *pita*. Today the dough is bought at the supermarket, and it has become very popular even in the States. Storebought phyllo results in extremely flaky, elegant pies. But the homemade dough has a more earthy, satisfying texture, which seems in harmony with the earthiness of the filling.

Makes 13–15 servings

1. Remember that when you make dough, the flour and water measurements are not fixed. You will learn how much you need by the feel of your hands on the dough. Starting with 1 cup of the all-purpose flour, mix in the whole wheat flour, salt, and baking powder; stir well. Add 1/2 cup of the beer-and-water mixture and stir well. Add the oil and mix again. Start adding the rest of the flour as needed until you have a dough that you can handle. This is a very light dough that feels good and pliable, not at all stiff.

2. Separate into 2 large, slightly unequal balls. Cover and let rest while you make the filling.

3. Wash the spinach and other greens, put them in a deep stew pot with just a cup of water, and place it over low heat to steam the greens and soften them. They will greatly reduce in volume. When the greens wilt, remove them from the heat and drain them.

4. Lift them with tongs a few at a time, wrap them in paper towels, and squeeze. You want them as dry as possible. Place them in the largest bowl you possess. Add the scallions, onion, leek, and herbs. Crumble the feta onto the greens and mix well. Grind the pepper over the greens and add 3 tablespoons olive oil. Beat the eggs lightly with the yogurt, add to the greens, and mix well.

5. Preheat your oven to 400°F.

6. To roll out the dough, clear a large work surface, like a kitchen table. Put cornstarch in a sifter and cover the surface with it. Place the larger ball of dough on this surface and press with your hands to form a circle. Then take an extra-long rolling pin and roll it over the dough repeatedly from the center to the sides, rotating the dough frequently, until the diameter of your circle of dough is about 24 inches. (If you plan to use a rectangular pan to bake the *pita*, you can shape the dough accordingly.)

7. Brush the bottom and sides of a 15-inch-diameter, 2-inch-deep pan with oil, roll the dough onto the rolling pin, and place it in the pan so that it covers the bottom and sides and hangs outside the rim. (For a large *pita* use a 16 x 11 x 2-inch pan.) Brush again with oil.

8. Add the filling—which must be cool, never hot—and then roll out the second ball of dough. This will be 2 inches smaller in diameter than the bottom crust. Roll it over the rolling pin and place it over the filling to cover. Crimp or roll the edges of the two crusts together into a decorative scroll, brush generously with oil, and score slits on top.

9. Bake for 50 minutes, or until the top browns nicely.

For the *horta* filling:

1/2 pound spinach

1/2 pound various greens—dandelions, chicory, chard, and the like

6–7 scallions, white parts with an inch of green, chopped, or more to taste

1 onion, chopped (optional)

1 leek, white part only, washed well and sliced in rings

2 tablespoons minced mint

4 tablespoons minced dill

1 pound feta

Freshly ground pepper

3 tablespoons olive oil

4 eggs

1/4 cup yogurt or sour cream

Chard and Other Greens with Croutons

Hórta me Psomákia

2 1-pound bunches Swiss chard

2 tablespoons sea salt

1/2 cup oil

1 cup cubes of day-old bread

Juice of 1/2 lemon

1 ounce Parmesan or Pecorino Romano cheese

Serves 4–6

1. Fill your deepest pot halfway with water and bring to a boil. Trim the chard stalks a bit, separate them from the leaves, and wash everything really well. Cut the stalks in one-inch lengths. To the boiling water add the salt and the chard stalks and cook for 5 minutes. Cut the chard leaves in thirds and add them to the pot, pushing them with a wooden spoon so that they become thoroughly immersed. Cook uncovered for 10 minutes, or until the stalks are just tender. Drain really well and keep warm in a deep bowl.

2. Heat the olive oil in a frying pan. When it starts smoking, toss all the bread cubes in the oil, stir until brown, and then pour the whole thing on top of the greens. Add the lemon juice to the pan, scrape, and pour onto the greens. Then grate the sharp cheese on the greens and serve immediately.

THE CHEESES OF GREECE

It was a golden, mild autumn when I finally visited my mother's birthplace in the mountainous region of Epirus, a place so filled with myths and thrilling stories of courage, resistance, and sacrifice that it was for me a nearly sacred journey. Who were the people who had given birth to my tragic mother—relatives, men and women I had never met? I can still see the *sousourádhas* (wagtails) outside our hotel window, sassy birds ingrained in our folklore, and smell the pines in the courtyard with their overwhelming, piercing scent.

In that mild October of memory we drove to Dodoni with its ancient amphitheater and I thought of Olympiás, the wild mother of Alexander, and of Persephónê, both goddess and mother. The late sun's rays glistened with silver undertones on the grey rocks of the amphitheater, a white light with shadows. The silence was filled with sounds that only the outdoors far from civilization allows us to hear—the bells on the throats of goats, the whistle of a bird, the mooing of a cow—and I was surrounded by the numinous, by ancient presence. I spoke to women walking behind their goat flocks as they returned them home, their hands never stopping in the spinning, spinning of wool on the spindle. I was at home, in peace, "surprised by joy." Is it any wonder, then, that I order all of my feta from Dodoni? It is creamy and rich without any of the sour aftertaste of supermarket feta.

This cheese, or a form of it, was known to the great Homer. When Odysseus arrives in the Cyclops's cave, he sees the laden shelves:

> The shelves were bent by the weight of the cheeses, and the pens crowded with lambs and kids. . . . the pots, jugs and well-crafted vessels used for milking were running over with the buttermilk. With passion then my friends begged me to take from the cheeses and run. . . . And after we lit a fire and made sacrifice, we ate from the cheeses, and sat waiting for him. . . .Cyclops [himself] sat down to milk the ewes and the she-goats who were bleating. . . . And, immediately, squeezing half of the milk he gathered it in knit baskets that he then placed on the shelves. The other half he poured in vessels so that he could have it with his evening meal.

Even Odysseus admits later that it would have been so much better had they grabbed the cheeses and run.

Down through the ages, the story of milk repeats itself: cheeses take their distinctive tastes from the milk—cow's, ewe's, goat's, or a blending of the three—and from their storage containers, which may be barrels, large tin cans, animal skins, or wax. During the Easter season, the soft cheeses of Greece are at their best and eaten with relish after the forty-day fast.

In addition to the familiar feta, which actually varies greatly from Greek region to region, there are other soft cheeses, some of them sold in specialty markets in the States.

The white *myzíthra* is a mild cheese made of all three kinds of milk, but low in fat and salt. Eaten with fruit and honey, it's like a dessert; that's how we liked it. Used in a *pita* (pie), it adds a piquancy all its own. Familiar to all the Balkans, *myzíthra* also comes in aged form, which is salty; this is the form sold in markets in the States. What makes it confusing is that *myzíthra* is also known by two other names: as *manoúri* in northern Greece and as *anthótyro* in Crete. As *anthótyro*, it is made of the creamiest cow's and ewe's milk combined. It is used in the traditional *kaltsoúnia* of Crete because of its sweetness.

Manoúri, known to American connoisseurs from specialty markets, is made of sour milk and cream from cow's milk and is white, soft, and dense. It comes in cylindrical form encased in cheesecloth and blends wonderfully with herbs and spices.

Haloúmi, a cheese from Cyprus, is now found in American supermarkets. The one sold here is salty and solid and has the distinction of not melting when heated. So it's excellent for *saganáki*, (see page 36)—fried cheese with a bit of lemon squeezed over it, eaten as an appetizer.

The final soft cheese I'll mention has the peculiar name of *kalatháki*, little basket. It is impressed with the interweave pattern of the basket in which it was traditionally stored and hung, reminiscent of Homer's description in the Cyclops's cave.

A form of soft cheese accompanies almost every meal in a Greek household.

The yellow, harder cheeses are many, some widely available, others reserved for those lucky ones who happen to visit the particular village or island. Such a visit I made during an early spring when the snow was still heavy on the mountains, in the elegant, traditionally built town of Metsovo in northern Epirus. They make a cheese there with a nutty, smoky flavor that I would put next to any French cheese of great fame. It comes in a cylinder encased in dark brown, and it is aged, delicious and rare, produced only in Metsovo and known as Metsovonê.

The two most familiar and most consumed yellow cheeses of Greece are the mild and delicious *kasséri* and the hard and sharp *kefalotýri*, more like Parmesan. They are found in good markets in the United States.

Eggplant with Feta

Melitzánes me Feta

There are so many ways to cook eggplant that it is difficult to choose which one to share. I find this recipe so much lighter than the familiar eggplant Parmesan that I hope you will try it. It is a truly delicious combination of flavors that will delight even those who don't like eggplant. (With thanks to my niece Natassa.)

4 small eggplants (2 pounds total)

4 tablespoons olive oil

1 onion, sliced

2 cloves garlic, chopped

1/2 pound feta, sliced

2 large ripe tomatoes, sliced

1 teaspoon ground pepper

4 basil leaves, torn, or 2 tablespoons snipped flat-leaf parsley

Serves 4

1. Preheat the broiler to 500°F.

2. The traditional preparation of eggplant, especially the thick purple ones, is to wash them, cut off the stem, and remove vertical strips of the skin so that you have parallel lines of white and purple on them. Some people don't like the slightly bitter skin; I happen to like it, but if you don't, you may peel the eggplants. Now cut them crosswise in 1/4-inch slices.

3. Pour 2 tablespoons oil onto a cookie sheet and place the eggplant on it, rubbing both sides of each slice in the oil. Pop the cookie sheet under the broiler and brown the eggplant on both sides. If you are grilling outside, you can brown them on the grill.

4. Now set the oven to 400°F.

5. Place the rest of the oil, onion slices, and garlic in a heavy frying pan and sauté until the onions are just turning to brown. Remove from heat and add the sliced feta on top of the onions; it will start to melt. Arrange eggplant slices in a baking dish; I use a 9 x 7 x 2-inch glass oval. Cover eggplant with onion-feta mixture, and then with the sliced ripe tomatoes.

6. Sprinkle with pepper (the feta provides the saltiness) and the basil or parsley, drizzle a bit of olive oil on top, and bake in the preheated oven for 25 minutes.

Stuffed Eggplant

Moussaká Papoutsákia

4 1/2-pound eggplants

4 tablespoons olive oil

For the filling:

4 tablespoons olive oil

1 1/2 pounds ground meat

1 large onion, chopped

1 cup red wine

1–2 garlic cloves, chopped

1 14.5-ounce can diced tomatoes, or several large ripe ones

1/4 cup snipped flat-leaf parsley

1 tablespoon dried oregano

1 tablespoon salt

1 tablespoon black pepper

For the béchamel:

2 cups warm milk

5 tablespoons melted butter

5 tablespoons all-purpose flour

Salt and pepper

Grated nutmeg (optional)

2 egg yolks

1/4 cup feta or Parmesan cheese

My husband was an officer in the army for the first seven years of our marriage, so we traveled across the United States. I looked for restaurants that, at that time, dared to have Greek food on the menu, but rarely found anything worth writing about. It took years of tourism in Greece for Greek dishes to be considered here in the States. One that became known was moussaka, but the American dish is such a rich, heavy version of the original that I will not eat it. At home in Greece, my family is known for its *moussaká*, especially the stuffed eggplant halves we call *papoutsákia*, "little shoes."

And it's not just me who has this opinion: When my college choir was on tour one year, I stayed in the home of a pastor who was planning to visit Greece. I gave him my parents' address, and they offered him a meal that left him rapturous. He wrote me from there, "Your mother makes the most superb moussaka imaginable." Of course.

Serves 8

1. Wash the eggplants and cut off the stems. Slice each eggplant in two lengthwise. Scoop out the pulp, leaving about 3/4 inch of flesh all around the eggplant half. If the pulp is too seedy, dump it; if not, chop it up and save for the béchamel. Brush the halves with the 4 tablespoons olive oil and broil them on both sides until soft. Place side by side in a large baking pan in which they fit snugly.

2. Now for the filling: In 4 tablespoons oil, brown the meat and onion together. Add the wine and stir. Add the garlic, tomatoes, parsley, oregano, salt, pepper, and 1/2 cup water. Bring to a boil and simmer until the liquids are absorbed.

3. Preheat oven to 375°F.

4. Now make the béchamel as my stepmother taught me to make it: Heat the milk first and keep it warm. Melt the butter in a heavy saucepan and stir the flour in with a whisk until butter is absorbed and starts to foam. Stirring constantly over low heat, gradually add the milk and let it turn the flour mixture creamy. Move from the heat source and add the seasonings. Beat the egg yolks in a bowl and start adding some of the hot béchamel. Then add the

tempered yolks to the saucepan and cook, stirring, until you have a consistency like firm custard; it has to be thick enough to form a cover over the stuffed eggplant.

5. Stuff the eggplant halves with the meat filling, creating little mounds. Cover these with the béchamel sauce, then spread crumbled feta or grated Parmesan on them and bake until the sauce turns golden brown, about 45 minutes. Serve hot.

Note: For lighter fare, especially in summer, don't use béchamel. Cover the eggplant with slices of large, ripe tomatoes, sprinkle them with bread crumbs and cheese, and bake as above.

Sweet Cheese Pies from Crete

Kaltsoúnia Krítis

You may encounter this recipe as *skaltsounia* also. Cretans have their own dialect, understood by most of us but unique in its pronunciation of consonants.

For this sweet you will need several soft cheeses. The Cretan recipe asks for a large amount of *anthótyro*, the much milder *myzíthra* of the island. Knowing how difficult it is to obtain in the United States, much less in bulk, I experimented with Greek and Italian cheeses, the latter very easily found in the market. The result was so successful with everyone who tasted them that I give you here my own recipe for *kaltsoúnia* filling. These are good with coffee, with breakfast, as dessert with fruit, for parties. You may want to experiment with substitutions, but this one is a sure bet. The dough for the crust is just right as is.

Makes about 22 pieces

1. Mix 2 cups flour with baker's ammonia (my preference) or baking powder. In a tilt-head stand mixer, whip softened butter with sugar; add yolks and whip some more. Now change the whip for the mixer's dough hook.

2. Add flour mixture alternately with milk until mixture forms a dough. Turn out on a floured surface and add more flour as needed. This is a very soft dough that can be extended just with the pressure of your hands or a light dowel. Let it rest while you prepare the filling.

3. Preheat the oven to 350°F.

4. Mix all filling ingredients together. Start with one egg white, and if mixture is too stiff, add the second one; the mixture must not be runny. You may reduce sugar by 1/4 cup if you don't want the *kaltsoúnia* very sweet.

5. Now roll the prepared dough flat to 20 inches in diameter and cut circles out of it (I have a metal ring 4 inches in diameter and this is what I use). Reroll the dough and repeat this process until the dough is used up. Place 1 tablespoon of filling in the middle, fold the dough over it, and seal by pressing with your fingers or the tines of a fork. Repeat.

6. Brush the pastries with 1 egg yolk thinned with 2 drops of cold water. Bake in the preheated oven for 30 minutes. You may want to sprinkle some cinnamon on top while the cheese pies are hot.

For the dough:

2 1/2 cups flour (approximate), plus more for kneading

1 teaspoon baker's ammonia (see note 1) or baking powder

1 stick butter, softened

1/2 cup sugar

2 egg yolks

1/2 cup milk

For the filling:

1/2 pound *manoúri* cheese (see note 2)

1/4 cup mascarpone

1/4 cup *kajmak* or clotted cream (see note 3)

1/4 cup ricotta

1–2 egg whites

1 cup sugar

1 egg yolk for glaze

Cinnamon (optional)

Note 1: Baker's ammonia has nothing to do with household ammonia. It was originally made of hart's horn, the antlers of the reindeer, and used in the manner we now use baking powder. In Greece we like it for making cookies; it gives a light texture to crisp cookies. It does have an ammonia smell before use, but it dissipates totally while baking. Use it only for rather small products, like cookies, not for cakes.

Note 2: *Manoúri* is a soft Greek cheese, found in specialty markets, with a slightly citrus flavor; you may substitute fresh mozzarella.

Note 3: *Kajmak* is like clotted cream. It is widely used in the Balkans and you will see a variety of spellings, but this spelling is used in my favorite market that specializes in Greek and Balkan products. Clotted cream can be found where English products are sold.

Sweet Cheese Pie in Phyllo
Glykiá Tyrópita

For the filling:

1/2 cup mascarpone

1/2 cup ricotta

1 cup fresh mozzarella

1/2 cup *kajmak* or clotted cream (see note 3 above)

1/4 cup sugar

1 egg

8–10 sheets of phyllo

1/2 stick butter, melted

For the syrup:

1/2 cup sugar

1/4 cup water

1 generous strip orange peel

1 teaspoon lemon juice

For inventive cooks, some wonderful recipes are born accidentally in the kitchen. I made *kaltsoúnia* for a reception and I had mascarpone, ricotta, and *kajmak* left over. These cheeses must be used up once the container is opened. I also had phyllo dough left over from making a dessert. But I needed something in place of *manoúri*, so I decided to experiment, using fresh mozzarella. This is the recipe that resulted, and it received praises from those who managed to eat it at the reception, since it disappeared quickly. When I make this now, I use an attractive pottery baking dish, so I can serve directly from it.

Note: Before working with phyllo, please see advice on its handling, page 14.

Makes 12 slices

1. Preheat the oven to 350°F.

2. Mix the three cheeses and the *kajmak* with the sugar and egg.

3. In a buttered baking dish measuring 11 x 9 x 2 inches, layer 4–5 phyllo sheets, buttering each. Add the cheese filling, then cover it with another 4–5 phyllo sheets, buttering the top sheet with particular care. Score the top and bake the sweet pie in the preheated oven for 30 minutes.

4. Meanwhile, boil the sugar, water, orange peel, and lemon juice. Let it reach 230°F, or syrup consistency, and then bring it to room temperature. When the pie is also at room temperature, pour this syrup on it and serve.

A Menu That Celebrates
the Earth at Pentecost

The Famous Greek Salad (*Horiátiki Saláta*) 85

Stuffed Eggplant (*Moussaká Papoutsákia*) 92
or for vegetarians, Greens in a Pie (*Hortópita*) 86

Stuffed Zucchini Flowers I (*Korfádhes Ghemistés*) 78

Sweet Cheese Pies from Crete (*Kaltsoúnia Krítis*) 95

Triangles of Cheese and Spinach (*Spanakotyropitákia*)

Spinach Pie in a Pan (*Spanakópita tou Tapsioú*)

Zucchini Fritters (*Kolokythokeftédhes*)

Peasant Bread (*Horiátiko Psomí*)

Eggplant in Rich Sauce (*Imám Bayildí*)

Artichokes and Potatoes (*Anghináres a la Políta*)

Chard and Other Greens in Red Sauce (*Kokkinistá Hórta*)

Yogurt Sauce (*Yiaoúrti Saltsa*)

Meat Patties on the Grill (*Soutzoukákia sti Skhára*)

Skewered Meat on the Grill (*Souvlákia sti Skhára*)

Potatoes with Oregano (*Patátes Riganátes*)

Yogurt Mousse (*Yiaoúrti Glykó, Afráto*)

Yogurt Dessert with Fruit Preserves (*Yiaoúrti me Glyká Koutalioú*)

Almond Cookies I (*Amygdalotá*)

Almond Cookies II (*Amygdalotá*)

Quince Preserves (*Kydhóni Glykó*)

Chapter 4

THE PENTECOST SEASON CONTINUES: SUMMER

The country I knew as a child has changed since tourists discovered Greece as a summer playground. Their invasion has been good for the economy but sometimes hurtful to the land, the monuments, and even the culture. The people of the land withstood the ravages of war but have not done as well with rampant materialism. Still, there are thousands of tourists who respect the history of this remarkable small country and are profoundly grateful when they have a chance to get to know and eat with a Greek family. They discover then what Greek hospitality and joie de vivre mean.

❧ UNDER THE *PLÁTANOS* TREE ❧

The traditional liturgical color for most major Christian churches in the Pentecost season is green. Liturgical colors are more strictly observed in the Western than the Eastern churches, but the meaning of green is obvious—new life in both the church and nature. The heat becomes intense every summer in Greece and, coupled with dry weather and fierce winds, it has resulted in terrible fires in recent years. The precious and limited forests of the Greek countryside have suffered through the centuries, but for those who love and respect nature, each green pine tree is a treasure. I remember my father breathing deeply whenever we traveled to the country from the city and thanking God aloud for every breeze that wafted the smell of the pine toward him.

The country is blessed with pines but also with huge plane trees that grow near water. The plane tree lives for a long time and has branches loaded with very large leaves the shape of maple leaves. It is so beloved of Greeks, this *plátanos* of song and myth, that it has entered our historic consciousness and storytelling. On the island of Kos, in the town square, locals will show you a tremendous *plátanos* reputed to have been there since the time of Hippocrates. Such myths of longevity abound for both the *plátanos* and olive tree. In almost every village square there is a large *plátanos* throwing a blessedly cool shadow in which people gather and sit around bare square tables, talk, or play backgammon. In Pelion, in the summer, all our children together could enter the cavelike shelter of a tremendous *plátanos*. One of those trees has a small chapel within its embrace. Under such trees thousands of meals have been eaten and enjoyed.

My dear friend Aliki has a lovely home overlooking the bay at the charming town of Kamena Vourla, in Thessaly. Her villa, surrounded by both decks and a yard, is perfect for outdoor meals but, even so, we took a picnic under a village *plátanos* that last summer of my father's life. Nearby was a stone cistern that never stopped gushing water descending from the mountains and, inside the deep stone sink under it, we placed the bottles of beer to keep them cold. Aliki's aunt, a superb cook, had assembled a feast for us, and there we sat under the *plátanos* to eat an unforgettable meal. The vegetables were fresh and green, and the memory of it all has a perfection that has proved unequaled. Some of the indispensible recipes for eating under the *plátanos* tree in your own green getaway follow.

Triangles of Cheese and Spinach

Spanakotyropitákia

These are similar to *tyropitákia* (page 15), but they are larger and contain spinach, scallions, and oil instead of butter. *Spanakotyropi-tákia* make an excellent first course with or without a salad.

Note: Before working with phyllo, please see advice on its handling, page 14.

Makes 20 triangles

1. Preheat the oven to 350°F.

2. Mix filling ingredients well together. "Knead" with wooden spoons to soften the spinach somewhat. (This filling is much thicker than the one for the flat *pitas*.)

3. Brush one sheet of phyllo with oil, folding it twice lengthwise; brush the top surface of this 13 x 3-inch strip with oil. Put a tablespoon of filling on the narrow edge and fold as described for the *tyropitákia* (page 15), the way a flag is folded. The resulting triangle will measure 3 inches on each side. Place on a cookie sheet, seam side down, and brush the top with oil. Repeat until phyllo and filling are used up.

4. Bake for 30 minutes, or more if needed.

For the filling:

1 10-ounce package prewashed baby spinach

10 ounces feta, crumbled

4 scallions, chopped

2 tablespoons snipped parsley

4 tablespoons snipped dill weed

2 leaves mint, shredded

1 heaping tablespoon sour cream

1 egg, lightly beaten

1 tablespoon olive oil

1/2 pound phyllo

Oil, for the phyllo

Spinach Pie in a Pan

Spanakópita tou Tapsioú

For the filling:

10 ounces organic prewashed baby or dark spinach

7–8 scallions, white part with an inch of green, finely diced

1 leek, white part only, well washed and diced

1/4 cup snipped fresh dill weed

1 sprig mint (about 4 leaves), shredded

Salt and pepper, to taste

1 pound feta, crumbled (see note)

4 eggs, slightly beaten

1/4 cup thick sour cream

3 tablespoons olive oil

Olive oil for brushing on phyllo, about 1 cup

1/2 pound phyllo, brought to room temperature

No season of the Greek year is without its version of a *pita*. The one that is always appropriate, always welcome, is spanakopita. I remember being apprehensive the first time I served it to American guests, thinking it might be too exotic for them, and one charming guest asking me if the greens were collards. I was pleasantly surprised at their reaction, and since then it has been a winner not only at my table but with my daughters' college friends. It was a good day, they said, when Mama brought spanakopita to school.

I have to confess that if there is one dish I am proud of, it is this one. I have tried many variations through the years, but this is the best and most elegant of the lot.

Here, unlike in most of this book's recipes using phyllo, the dough is brushed with oil instead of butter. Some Greek cooks use only olive oil with phyllo; I prefer oil with fillings that include greens and scallions, butter with feta and egg fillings or desserts.

Note: Before working with phyllo, please see advice on its handling, page 14.

Makes 15 portions

1. In a large bowl place the prewashed spinach—a great time and labor saver. Add scallions, leek, herbs, salt (optional: feta is salty), and pepper, and mix. Stir in the crumbled feta and the eggs, then fold in the sour cream. Mix thoroughly. Add the 3 tablespoons olive oil and with two wooden spoons "knead" this mixture thoroughly. Let it sit so that the spinach almost wilts. (Plan to use the filling immediately, so it does not become watery.)

2. Preheat the oven to 350°F.

3. Pour good olive oil in a bowl; I will say what the Greeks say about some measurements: as much as it takes—*óso párei*. Have a pastry bush ready, and a greased metal baking pan about 12 x 9 x 2 inches. Place the sheets of phyllo in the pan one by one, lightly brushing each with oil. Remember, you don't have to cover every inch; the oil will diffuse in the baking.

4. After you build up 10 sheets of phyllo, spread the filling evenly on top of them. The filling will reduce greatly in volume as it bakes. Cover with the remaining 10 sheets from the package, brushing with oil as you go. Brush the top one thoroughly. Score into diamond or square shapes halfway to the bottom of the pan. To make diamonds, score first longitudinally, 2 inches apart, and then diagonally. Now dip your fingers into cold water and sprinkle the top so that the phyllo doesn't curl.

5. Bake in the preheated oven for about 40 minutes or until golden brown.

Note: For the table, I buy feta from a Greek website. For the filling here, you may use the packaged blocks of feta sold in supermarkets; avoid the crumbled kind. In general, however, best results are achieved by using the best quality of ingredients available.

Zucchini Fritters

Kolokythokeftédhes

3 8-ounce zucchini

4 scallions, finely sliced

1 cup plain bread crumbs

1/2 cup grated feta or a hard, aged cheese

1/2 cup snipped dill weed

2 mint leaves, shredded

1 egg

Salt and freshly ground black pepper, to taste

1/2 cup flour

Olive oil for frying

Lemon juice

The days we spent on the island of Naxos were filled with the discovery of a different beach each day and then a new restaurant each night. I remember one in particular because of its deliciously light zucchini fritters. They called them zucchini *keftédhes*, the word used for meatballs. Any mixture that results in a ball that can be fried usually carries this nomenclature. But they were fritters, the kind that melt in the mouth and are perfectly accompanied by yogurt or *skordhaliá*.

In the summer, when zucchini is so tender and plentiful, this makes for a surprisingly good appetizer. If you have a deep fryer, this recipe may turn out best.

Makes 20 fritters

1. When working with zucchini, make sure you let them get rid of their excess water. I shred my zucchini in a food processor, then place them in a colander, generously sprinkled with coarse salt to draw out the liquids. Let them sit for an hour. If they still feel wet, wrap them in a towel and squeeze.

2. Place the shredded zucchini in a large bowl. Mix the scallions, bread crumbs, grated cheese, dill, mint, egg, and salt into the zucchini. Grind pepper over the mixture. Check the consistency and add enough flour to give it solidity; you don't want a runny mixture, so adjust the flour accordingly. I use the flour chiefly for coating the fritters before frying.

3. Shape the fritters, place on baking sheet, cover with waxed paper, and chill them for an hour before frying.

4. Heat enough olive oil to come halfway up the fritters. Fry them on both sides, just a few at a time, so they will become crisp. Drain on paper towels.

5. For extra zing I sprinkle a bit of lemon juice on them. Serve hot with plain yogurt, *tzatzíki* (page 62), or *skordhaliá* (page 51).

THE MEANING OF ORDINARY BREAD

One summer when my husband served in Vietnam, I decided, young and worried as I was, to return to Greece, to live at home. That was the year I recaptured the meaning of being Greek. I had been away so long, starting with my impressionable late teens, that I had become more American than Greek. When a cousin made fun of my accent, I listened to myself, looked at myself, and decided that I liked being Greek. So I started paying attention, a quality I came to value even more than formal education. I paid attention to the people around me, to how they talked, and what they ate.

I thrilled to walk again into a bakery, to smell the yeasty goodness of it, and to break a warm loaf of bread with my hands before giving it to my child. Bread is so holy in the Greek memory that I observed with emotion a woman who worked for us pick up a piece of bread that had fallen on the floor; she blew on it and kissed it. "You must never throw bread away without kissing it," she told me. Years later I read Patrick Leigh Fermor's description in *Roumeli* of his war years with the Greek resistance fighters in the mountains of Crete. The fierce warriors would make the sign of the cross, he remembered, before eating the bread on those wild mountains they called their own, a bread so hard that it had to soak in milk before it could be eaten. Then, before they put the leftover pieces of bread away, "they would kiss them in memory of the Mystic Feast."

I think of this bread as metaphor for life and its universal essence as I knead my dough. Remembered visits to public ovens and the marvelous dark texture of peasant bread and its aroma keep me company as my hands move.

That summer when I became Greek again, I rented a house at a seaside village for us, and I befriended a big, good-looking girl with golden eyes, Chrysoula. Her eyes reminded me of the Greek classic novel *The Schoolmistress with the Golden Eyes*. It is a sad story, and this young bride also made me sad when I contemplated her fate with a domineering mother-in-law and a swaggering husband.

In the mornings Chrysoula would pass by my window, reminding me of a Greek goddess. She carried a long wooden tray on her shoulder, and in its compartments rose four loaves of bread. At noon I went with her to the baker's oven to retrieve these same loaves. The bread was sweet and dark, and my daughter, Niki, still thinks it was the best bread in the world. Whenever I remember its taste, I think of Chrysoula, my Greek roots, and friends I made.

As I watch the yeasty dough rising, I think about wheat and the scorched earth as the enemies rushed over it in my own country and so many others, about the deliberate effort of the conquerors to starve the conquered, to deprive them of bread, and again I stand in awe at the power of the human spirit to survive and rise again.

So start your day under your own tree and its shadows, with good bread from your oven. Have cheeses available and cool lettuce and cucumbers with only salt for dressing. And don't forget the olives!

Peasant Bread

Horiátiko Psomí

Because the season of Pentecost is also called "ordinary time" in liturgical language, I think of this as ordinary bread.

Makes 4 loaves

1. In 1 cup very warm (110°F) water, dissolve the yeast together with the 2 tablespoons flour and sugar. Cover and let it proof.

2. In a very large bowl mix the whole wheat flour and 2 cups bread flour with the salt; open a hole in the middle, and in it pour the dissolved yeast. Mix well. Combine the honey with 2/3 cup warm water and stir it in, followed by another cup of warm water. Add another cup of flour and the olive oil. Now add enough flour to form the dough.

3. Knead very well until the dough is shiny. Cover with a towel and let it rise in a warm place, free of drafts, until doubled in size. Punch down, let it rest, and then divide the dough in four, and start shaping the loaves. Place them in greased, metal loaf pans and let them rise again.

4. Preheat the oven.

5. Score the top of the loaves in three places and brush them with egg white. Bake at 400°F for 10 minutes, then reduce the temperature to 350°F and bake another 30 minutes. The bottom should sound hollow when thumped.

6. Let the bread cool for 10 minutes before slicing.

2 tablespoons granulated yeast

2 tablespoons all-purpose flour

2 tablespoons sugar

2 cups whole wheat flour

4 cups bread flour or unbleached flour (more if needed)

1 1/2 tablespoons kosher salt

1/3 cup honey

1/4 cup olive oil

1 egg white

❧ Fresh Vegetables of the Season ☙

One of the most delightful results of finally paying attention to our earth is the proliferation of farmers' markets in small towns and large. And while I think about it, let me give you the etymology of "ecology," originally spelled "oikology." The Greek word for home is *oikos*, the place where one lives, and the earth (our universe) is called *oikouméne*. The Greek diphthong omicron-iota (*oi*) is pronounced as *ee* in modern Greek; the spelling in English has been simplified by changing the *oi* into *e*, hence "ecumenical" (the inclusion of many denominations in one group) and "ecology" (the study of where we live—our earth home).

Shopping at farmers' markets takes me back to the produce markets of my childhood and the delightful street markets of many European cities. I'll always remember the smell of green vegetables in open crates, wet and cool in the early morning light, and the chant of the vendor, uninhibited, melodic, well projected as though the street were the stage of this actor in real life, the small farmer selling the results of his hands' labor.

Eggplant in Rich Sauce

Imám Bayildí

Two vegetables used in endless variations in Greece, where they are plentiful, are the eggplant and the artichoke. Showcasing the former, this recipe was cooked on the stovetop by my mother, and I prefer it to the baked method that many favor these days. Very slender eggplant is needed for this dish, which can be enjoyed hot or, as the Greeks enjoy it best, cold.

For me, the predominant memory evoked by this recipe is my father's wonderful laughter as he acted out the meaning of the name it carries, for the name is definitely Turkish, and the heavy Anatolian richness is undoubted. It is called *imám bayildí* and I assure you this is not Greek. An imam is a religious leader. Well, the imam liked this dish so much when his wife made it that he swooned; he fainted dead away (*bayildí*). Like all legends, it has its variations—he overate, or he was horrified by the expense of it all.

Whatever the cause of his swooning, the recipe is so heavy in its original version that you would have *bayildí* also. I will give you modified amounts of ingredients. This dish is tasty and aromatic, and richly evocative of Anatolia.

4 long, slender eggplants

1 cup snipped flat-leaf parsley

1 teaspoon each salt and pepper

4–6 garlic cloves, peeled and minced, or to taste

1/2 cup good olive oil

1 large onion, sliced in slender strips

4–6 ripe tomatoes, peeled and chopped

1–2 teaspoons sugar

1/2 teaspoon ground cinnamon

Serves 4

1. After you wash the eggplants and cut off the ends, slice off the skin lengthwise in alternating strips about 1/2 inch in width. On each skinless strip, run a sharp knife to open 2 to 4 long, pocket-like slits. Combine the parsley, salt and pepper, and garlic and stuff the slits with this mixture. Heat the oil in a skillet and brown the eggplants lightly on all sides. Remove them to a casserole fit for the stovetop.

2. Sauté the onions in the skillet, then add the tomatoes, sugar, and cinnamon and cook for about 5 minutes.

3. Pour the tomato mixture over the eggplants. Set the casserole over low heat, cover it, and simmer for half an hour. Add water only as needed. Check for tenderness and cook a bit longer if eggplant is not sufficiently soft.

4. Arrange the eggplant on a platter with the sauce. Serve with peasant bread, *horiátiko psomí* (crusty country bread), and good feta.

❧ THE FASCINATING ARTICHOKE ❧

During the lean years, the artichoke was a substitute for meat in Greece. The arti-choke belongs to the family of thistles, which are plentiful on the dry mountainsides of Greece. The edible bulb (known as cardoon) has been cultivated from ancient times and is native to the Mediterranean region. Sources agree that the cultivated artichoke originated in Sicily, which was an ancient Greek colony. However, it seems not to have entered European cuisines before the seventeenth century. It is natu-ral, then, because of its long existence and availability, that the Greeks and Italians should excel in the preparation of the artichoke. Keep in mind that most Greek and Italian recipes are for *baby* artichokes, which are very fresh, available at the begin-ning of the season, and have not had time to develop the troublesome choke. If you have a friend who cultivates them, see what a difference it makes to use baby arti-chokes instead of the large ones. Here is a simple way to prepare large artichokes whole for a variety of recipes and sauces:

Cut 2 lemons in half. Squeeze the juice into a pan of cold, salted water. Cut off the woody stems of the artichokes. Remove all the hard outer leaves. Now open the artichoke from the top by pushing the remaining leaves out of the way like a flower, and with a spoon scoop out the choke. Rub the leaves with the lemon halves, then drop them in the lemon water until ready to use.

Artichokes and Potatoes

Anghináres a la Políta

The following recipe is a classic, known by everyone in Greece as *anghináres a la Políta* (artichokes cooked the way the women of Constantinople cooked them).

First an apology: My littlest grandchild told me one day, "Mika, you are homemade." Knowing his penchant for interesting phrases, I waited. "I mean you make everything from scratch," he explained, his eyes shining. So my apology to my sweet Miles for not doing this one from scratch. I use canned or frozen artichoke hearts for this recipe, but you may use the real thing if you can find the tender ones in the market. This is a satisfying main or side dish, not just for vegetarians.

3 14-ounce cans of artichoke hearts (or you may use fresh)

1/4 cup olive oil

1 onion, chopped

6 scallions, chopped

12 new white potatoes, in their skins or peeled, cut in two

3 carrots, sliced in rounds

Juice of 1–2 lemons

Salt and pepper

1/2 cup snipped dill weed

Serves 12

1. Rinse the artichokes well under cold water to get rid of the canning liquid.

2. In a large, heavy frying pan, heat the oil on medium heat and sauté the onions and scallions. Add the potatoes and stir to coat them well. Add the carrots. Now add the well-rinsed artichokes and 2 cups warm water. Pour the lemon juice over everything. Salt and pepper to taste.

3. Cover and simmer for 1 hour if using fresh artichokes, 30 minutes if canned. In the last 5 minutes, add the dill.

4. Serve hot or cold. I like this dish just as it is, flavorful and light, smelling of summer. But for something fancier, serve with *avgolémono* when hot, or with yogurt sauce or *tzatzíki* when cold.

Chard and Other Greens in Red Sauce

Kokkinistá Hórta

2 pounds chard, or a combination of available greens

4 scallions, sliced

1/2 cup olive oil, divided

1 teaspoon sea salt

2 young zucchini, or any vegetable you find in your fridge

2 tomatoes, peeled

Parsley and dill, snipped (about 1/4 cup combined)

Salt and pepper, to taste

2 cups bread cubes from homemade bread

Juice of 1/2 lemon

Grated cheese (optional)

The word *kokkinistá*—from *kokkino*, red— found in many Greek recipes refers to a sauce that contains tomatoes and their juice, which together render that lovely red color to sauces. This falls in the category of quick, easy, and delicious. A perfect, light lunch dish.

Serves 4

1. Wash your greens, leaving them wet. Sauté the scallions in 1/4 cup olive oil over medium heat. After 3 minutes add the greens, cut up, together with their stems. Push them down with the lid so that they fit (I use my copper frying pan for this recipe). Add sea salt. Cover and let them simmer in their own liquid.

2. Meanwhile, if you have a couple of young zucchini, yellow squash, or some broccoli, slice them and add them to the greens. Cut the peeled tomatoes or grate them and add them to the pan. Add the herbs, and season to taste. Now cover and let everything wilt. It won't take long, about 10 minutes, so don't go away.

3. Watch the fresh tomatoes; when they look no longer firm but wilted, remove everything with tongs and place in a bowl.

4. In the same frying pan, heat the remaining 1/4 cup of oil and toss the bread cubes in it over high heat, continuing to stir briskly even after the oil has been absorbed. Keep at it until the bread looks slightly brown on the edges. Toss the bread onto the greens and then squeeze the half lemon over everything. You may enjoy some grated cheese on the greens also.

Yogurt Sauce

Yiaoúrti Saltsa

This sauce, white and rich, is good with *kokkinistá hórta* (page 112), *anghináres a la políta* (page 111), and *imám bayildí* (page 109), especially if you make the vegetable your whole meal.

Makes 2 cups
Mix all ingredients well and refrigerate covered. Serve cold.

1 cup Greek yogurt

1 cup sour cream

2 tablespoons snipped dill (optional)

A few drops of olive oil

Salt and pepper, to taste

❧ Cool Yogurt ❧
Filled with Benefits—and Possibilities

You may have noticed that all the recipes in this section may be enhanced by cool yogurt. What is this wonderful substance and why is it so ingrained in the Greek diet? My American husband grew up drinking cold milk as his calcium source. When he returned home after a year in Vietnam, he told me that cold milk was what he missed the most in his diet. In Greece, after our mothers weaned us, we rarely drank milk, especially cold, but we did not lack for calcium. Two dairy products are never absent from Greek tables—feta cheese and yogurt, bought fresh daily.

In the Greece of my childhood, each neighborhood was self-sufficient. Young tykes would be sent on grocery runs while the mother stood on the home's balcony and watched. On one corner was the butcher, across from him the grocer, and next to him the wine shop, smelling of vinegar as one passed by, since both vinegar and wine were bought on draft. At the other end, the baker's oven filled the street with wondrous aromas of the staff of life. Midway sat the little produce stand with parsley, dill, lettuce, cucumbers, and tomatoes, the dew still beady on their green freshness.

Another corner held the dairy store. Everything there was in glass cases. It smelled of warm milk and that luscious cream produced only by ewe's milk. Rows of colorful pastries, exquisite designs of roasted almonds on top and filled with *crema Chantilly*, and the delicately flavored custards among flaky layers of phyllo. Unbelievable numbers of calories lay dormant in their gastronomic beauty.

In an adjoining glass case was the yogurt. It came in various sizes of *giouvétsi*, simple round earthenware crocks, probably used from time immemorial. The yogurt they contained was thick enough to hold a spoon upright, and there was *kaimáki* on the top, the rich cream that could be peeled off like a cover. The yogurt was not sweet, never mixed with fruit, never runny; it was a product perfected through the ages to be eaten plain or to accompany a variety of vegetables, rarely sweets.

Who discovered its multiple uses and benefits? When I first started writing, years ago, Greek yogurt was fairly new in the United States. In the Balkans, however, it seems to have existed forever. The Greeks, naturally, claim that the ancients discovered it as they saw what the sun did to milk that was left outside. The Turks say they discovered it when they were nomads; milk in gourds or goatskins turned into yogurt as the camels swayed their bodies in the endless desert. The fact remains that the best yogurt, for a long time, was found in the Balkans, and it was the milk that made the difference. (Now, one can find good, thick yogurt in supermarkets—Fage, Oikos, Chobani, and the Greek Gods are very good products.) Now that yogurt is so popular, we know that a variation of this marvelous dairy product is found in almost all cultures in infinite varieties and nomenclature. Doctors these days are emphasizing the benefits of probiotics, which tend to be quite expensive in pill or powder form; it is much cheaper to let the yogurt bacteria give us the same benefits.

There is no limit to the recipes one can create with this white and delicious substance. The Greeks claim medicinal powers for it—that it helps with intestinal problems, that it averts or reduces hangover. Others attribute their longevity to the daily consumption of yogurt. I remember that Mother would lather us with it when we were sunburned.

I think of its beneficial properties more during the summer than in the winter months because it is cool and low in calories. Most of what I do with yogurt has resulted accidentally in the kitchen. One spring, when those lovely plump English peas appeared in the market, I cooked them in the traditional sauce (see *arakás me sáltsa*, page 13). Then I put them in the refrigerator to cool and served them later in the day. I put some plain yogurt on the same plate and mixed them as I ate. Feelings and memories of childhood summers rushed through me so forcefully that I knew it was the first time in decades I had hit upon this once familiar combination. This can be done with several cooked vegetables, with zucchini, beets, carrots. They must be cold to mix well with yogurt.

So think of yogurt when you think of vegetables. The two go beautifully together. But yogurt also goes well with some meats; otherwise, why would the ubiquitous gyro be so popular in countries outside Greece? Here I offer a couple of recipes I consider better than gyro—*soutzoukákia* and the more familiar souvlaki—that you can grill at home and serve with yogurt sauces.

Meat Patties on the Grill

Soutzoukákia sti Skhára

1 pound ground meat

4 scallions, finely chopped

1 teaspoon cumin

1/4 cup snipped parsley

Salt and pepper

2 tablespoons oregano

Juice of 1 lemon

1/4 cup olive oil

Soutzoukákia are delicious with plain yogurt or *tzatzíki*, with any vegetable or salad, or in place of hamburgers. When you cannot grill outside, these also cook well on a flat pancake griddle.

Serves 6

1. Mix the meat, scallions, cumin, parsley, and salt and pepper to taste. Shape into 6 oblong patties. Sprinkle them generously with oregano.

2. To make a *ladholémono* for basting, whip together the lemon juice and olive oil until cloudy.

3. Grill the patties over hot coals or gas at medium-high heat, basting often, or at least twice on each side. Five minutes on each side should be sufficient.

Skewered Meat on the Grill

Souvlákia sti Skhára

For souvlaki (plural *souvlákia*) you may use beef, pork, lamb, or chicken. Do try it with excellent lamb. It is better known here as shish kebab. For such an occasion, you need to plan ahead.

Serves 6

1. Mix together the marinade ingredients in a jar.

2. Cut beef, pork, lamb, or chicken into bite-size pieces and place in a bowl. Shake the marinade and pour over the meat. Cover well and refrigerate for several hours.

3. As the fire on the grill heats up, drain the marinade and thread the meat and the colorful vegetables alternately on 6 skewers. Each skewer should contain 1 garlic clove, 3 pieces of meat, 3 mushrooms, 3 tomatoes, and equal slices of onion, zucchini, and peppers of each color. Sprinkle with oregano.

4. Whip together the oil and lemon juice. While the skewers are on the fire, baste often with this mixture.

5. Serve *souvlákia* with *tzatzíki*.

For the marinade:

1/2 cup olive oil

2 tablespoons lemon juice

4 garlic cloves, peeled and crushed

2 tablespoons oregano

1 bay leaf

Salt and pepper

For the skewers:

2 pounds meat of choice, cubed

3 peppers (1 each green, red, and yellow), cut in 1-inch squares

1 red onion, cut in 1-inch squares

18 cherry tomatoes or tomato chunks

18 mushrooms

2 zucchini, cut in 1/2-inch slices

6 large garlic cloves, peeled

Oregano for sprinkling

For basting:

1/4 cup olive oil

Juice of 1 lemon, strained

Potatoes with Oregano

Patátes Riganátes

6 large potatoes, preferably Yukon Gold

1/4 cup olive oil

1 lemon, halved

2 tablespoons oregano

Salt and pepper

My family would be disappointed if I didn't give you the perfect starch accompaniment for grilled meats like *soutzoukákia* (page 116) and *souvlákia* (page 117). I came up with this quick and easy recipe to save on calories and because my children and grandchildren were never crazy about French fries. These potatoes are a great hit; you will enjoy both the aroma and the taste. They are good hot and cold.

Serves 10

1. Preheat the oven to 400°F.

2. Peel the potatoes and cut in wedges, like very thick fries. Spread them in a metal pan large enough to hold them in one layer. Drizzle with the olive oil and toss to coat. Sprinkle with the juice of 1/2 lemon and toss again. Sprinkle oregano on the potatoes and salt and pepper to taste.

3. Bake until the edges crisp, then turn the potatoes with a spatula and continue baking. After cooking about 30 minutes, taste one for doneness. Scrape the bottom of the pan with a spatula, and pile the potatoes on a platter or deep bowl. Taste and, if needed, add the rest of the lemon juice.

Yogurt Mousse

Yiaoúrti Glykó, Afráto

My niece Natassa, an accomplished cook, was enthusiastic about this dessert because of its simplicity, ease, and taste. These amounts are for a small group. When you have a party, double it if need be, especially as a cool finish to a barbecue in the summer.

I sometimes serve this with a grating of nutmeg. Also with Greek coffee powder (Greek coffee is highly pulverized); sprinkle half a teaspoon of the coffee in the yogurt just before serving. The best of all the toppings was shaved semisweet chocolate. Offer the toppings to the guests and let them choose.

32 ounces yogurt

Zest of 1 lemon

Juice of 1 lemon

1 14-ounce can condensed milk

Serves 10

Whip all the ingredients together and refrigerate for at least 4 hours before serving. It turns into a mousse.

Yogurt Dessert with Fruit Preserves

Yiaoúrti me Glyká Koutalioú

1 pound thick Greek yogurt

4 heaping tablespoons preserves

It was my dear friend Aliki who served me this dessert the first time. A decade later, in New York City, I was eating at the finest Greek restaurant of the city, Molyvos, next to Carnegie Hall. The dessert offering? Yogurt with preserves.

That summer afternoon at Aliki's, after a swim, lunch, and siesta, we were cooling off on the balcony under the grapevine's shadow. Aliki came out with bowls of white, wonderfully creamy yogurt, made locally. In it she swirled the most beautiful deep red, almost maroon cherry preserves. Fascinated, I watched the colors blend and change as the rich purple-red of the cherries in their syrup mixed with the thick whiteness of the yogurt to emerge like a Pollock painting. The taste of the tangy yogurt with the sweetness of the cherries was seductive. (I have also seen it done with honey and with just the syrup of sour cherries.) This is a cool, creamy, and utterly satisfying taste, nothing like the fruity yogurt you buy in the supermarket, so if you have friends who preserve whole fruit, try this. Molyvos offers it with quince preserves (see page 124). Sour cherry preserves like those Aliki offered, as well as quince and other fine fruit preserves, may be bought from a Greek market.

Serves 4

In each of four crystal bowls, place 1 cup yogurt, add 1 generous tablespoon preserves, and stir. Serve cold.

Almond Cookies I
Amygdalotá

These are like macaroons, and I don't know of another cookie that's as delicious and addictive.

Makes approximately 3 dozen

1. Preheat the oven to 400°F.
2. Put ground almonds, sugar, and egg whites in a food processor and pulse until well blended. Place spoonful by spoonful on a baking sheet covered with parchment paper. Press half an almond in the middle of each.
3. Bake for 10 minutes. The cookies will be barely rosy on the edges, soft in the middle. If you bake them too long, they will be good but very crisp.

1 1/2 cups very finely ground white almonds

1/2 cup sugar

3 egg whites

36 blanched almond halves

Almond Cookies II
Amygdalotá

1. Preheat the oven to 400°F.
2. Process first five ingredients together; almond paste is very stiff, so the processor is necessary. Drop the mixture on parchment paper one spoonful at a time in balls about 1 inch in diameter. Place an almond half in the middle of each mound and press the ball so it forms a pretty circle or oval. Leave space between the mounds; they do expand. Bake for 10 minutes.

1 can almond paste (8 ounces)

1 cup powdered sugar

1/3 cup ground almonds

5 tablespoons semolina flour

1 egg white

36 blanched almond halves

Quince Preserves

Kydhóni Glykó

4 quince fruit (2 pounds total)

2 tablespoons lemon juice

2 cups sugar

4 scented geranium leaves
(*arbarórizo* in Greek), or
4 large basil leaves

No one makes better quince "spoon sweet" (as Greeks call preserves) than my sister Doritsa. She would have a jarful ready for me to take back to the United States whenever I visited. I have tried to copy her recipe; mine is good but not quite as good as hers. Quince is rather rare in supermarkets, but when you find them, try this. They are in season in the fall, but I have been lucky to find them in a local market even in the summer.

Makes 2 pint jars of preserves

1. Peel the quince and remove seeds. This is easier said than done; use your best paring knife. Then cut in strips about the size of a matchstick, or grate them on the large holes of a grater.

2. For soft preserves: Place them in 3 cups water with 1 tablespoon lemon juice, and boil for 15 minutes. Add the sugar and stir. Add the scented geranium or basil leaves and cook until the fruit turns a lovely coral color and the aroma fills the kitchen. Add 1 more tablespoon of lemon juice and seal in sterilized jars.

3. For crunchy (which I much prefer): Boil the fruit and sugar together right away in 3 cups water until the liquid becomes syrup. Then add the lemon juice and aromatic scented geranium leaves. After the syrup binds (as the Greeks call it) at 260°F, remove from the heat, stir, and store in sterilized jars.

A Menu for Early Summer

Chard and Other Greens in Red Sauce (*Kokkinistá Hórta*) 112

Skewered Meat on the Grill (*Souvlákia sti Skhára*) 117

Potatoes with Oregano (*Patátes Riganátes*) 118 *or* Artichokes and
Potatoes (*Anghináres a la Políta*) 111

Peasant Bread (*Horiátiko Psomí*) 107

Yogurt Mousse (*Yiaoúrti Glykó, Afráto*) 119

Almond Cookies (*Amygdalotá*) 123

Sundried Tomatoes in Batter
(*Tomátes Kourkoúti*)

Omelet for Summer Lunch
(*Oméleta me Soutzoúkia*)

Greek Omelet for Two
(*Oméleta me Tomátes*)

Fresh Green Beans in Sauce
(*Fasolákia Fréska*)

Shrimp with Feta in a Pan
(*Gharídhes Saganáki*)

Cold Fish with Mayonnaise
(*Psári Mayonnaíza*)

Homemade Mayonnaise

Beet and Potato Salad
(*Rossikí Saláta*)

Sour Cherry Drink
(*Vissinádha*)

Fresh Lemonade
(*Lemonádha*)

Cool, Creamy, and Fruity Trifle

Tart with Cream and Cherries
(*Toúrta me Kerásia*)

Chapter 5

THE PENTECOST SEASON RIPENS:
LATE SUMMER

*S*ummer used to be the season when the village Greeks made money to help them exist the rest of the year. They used to rent the upstairs of their humble homes to the city folks while they moved downstairs to unfinished rooms that were spotlessly clean even when they had only dirt for a floor. I admired those villagers immensely for their resourcefulness and their endurance. Knowing how to utilize the resources of nature, however meager, is what saved them. Invariably, in one corner of their front room, they would burn a wick floating in a glass of oil in front of an icon of the Virgin. Summer is her season in Greece, and she is never forgotten.

BRIGHTENING THE SUMMER DOLDRUMS

Before we bid *adío* to summer, let's look at August, which, admittedly, is not a greatly loved month by city Greeks. The urbanites leave for the islands and the countryside; swimmers even avoid the sea in August, since it can get so hot. One great religious holiday comes at midmonth, a celebration of the Virgin Mary in all kinds of manifestations of adoration, with special attention to the miraculous. On August 15 everyone who is named Maria, and they are legion, celebrates her name day. The island of Tinos in the Cyclades is especially dedicated to Mary's love and worship, with sick people flocking to the place in August, since an icon of the Virgin (reminiscent of Roman Catholic Lourdes) is reputed to have miraculous powers there.

What makes this day doubly significant is once again the tight connection between church and state. On this day in 1940, while it was still in peacetime, the Greek light cruiser *Elli* was torpedoed by an Italian submarine. She had been lying at anchor off Tinos in honor of the religious celebration of the Dormition of the Virgin. The Greeks never forgot that insult by the Fascists of Mussolini, the megalomaniac whose ambition was to surpass Hitler and to reclaim the Roman Empire. A couple of months later, the Greeks would remember the *Elli* when Mussolini tried to invade their country.

On the whole, the Greek Orthodox wear their religion lightly, but those who put great emphasis on miracles and icons are quite convinced that power resides in icons, saints, and relics to a degree that, to the rest of us on the outside, approaches magic. Whatever one thinks or believes on this issue, August 15, the Dormition of the Virgin, is one of the most significant Greek holidays, giving a kind of centrality to an otherwise boring month. The faithful in years past also fasted during this season. (It should be noted that the farmers, however, consider August their best month, much of it having to do with the harvest of grapes and figs.)

Tinos is one of the Greek islands that, despite the prevailing Orthodox presence, retain the lingering influence of the Roman Catholic Venetians who occupied the Cyclades for many centuries. Tinos is not only central to the Orthodox love of Mary but also to a long-term Jesuit presence in Greece. Many years ago it was my great pleasure to visit Tinos in order to research an article on Catholic nuns who minister to poor girls of the islands and train them in traditional crafts. What stays with me is the beauty of the Orthodox church dedicated to Panayía (Mary), a white edifice that looks like a rectangular wedding cake. Inside, it was filled with hundreds of votive offerings. And once again, as I do whenever I visit rural Greece, I had the feeling that I was straddling the centuries, and that I was living among the ancients who never failed to thank their gods with votive offerings. All over the interior one saw replicas of hands, arms, legs, and other body parts, hammered in gold or silver, hanging from the ceiling, testaments of some long-ago healing.

Driving through the island I saw hundreds of the most elaborate dovecotes, like little houses—little castles for the birds—something I had not encountered in other parts of Greece. Wild birds are a delicacy in Greece, and I was appalled while reading through the famous cookbook by Tselementés (see page 26) to see recipes not only for hen, turkey, duck, and goose but also for squab, woodcock, partridge, thrush, quail, pheasant, turtledove, and guinea hen. Then I contemplated my own hypocrisy in eating some birds, like chicken and turkey, and not others, and decided not to say anything more about it.

Tinos, in addition to doves, is known for its pork products, especially sausages, and for its milk and soft cheeses. It is also famous for sundried tomatoes.

Sundried Tomatoes in Batter

Tomátes Kourkoúti

20 dried tomato halves

1 1/2 cups all-purpose flour

1/2 onion, cut very fine

2 tablespoons snipped
flat-leaf parsley

2 tablespoons cut-up fennel
fronds or dill (see note)

1 tablespoon salt

1 tablespoon pepper

Olive oil for frying

Greece is so blessed with sunlight that many cooks, longing to keep the summer freshness of fruits and vegetables, dry them in the sun to preserve them—a contrast to the practice in the American South, where I have lived for such a long time and where the fruits and vegetables are preserved by canning. For drying, the tomatoes are cut in half and salted very generously before being laid out in the sun for nearly two weeks, easy to do in sunny Greece. Then with twine and a large needle they are threaded together in long strips and hung in the sun to dry totally. For storing they are placed in cotton sacks and hung in a dark cool place. When cooks use them later in the year, they have to soak the sundried tomatoes first.

This marvelous recipe for battered sundried tomatoes is an appetizer said to be traditional to the island of Tinos.

Makes 20 appetizers

1. Soak the tomatoes in water until they swell up.

2. Mix flour, onion, parsley, and fennel or dill with salt and pepper in a bowl. Add enough water to create a thick batter.

3. Drain and rinse the tomatoes, cut them into thirds, and stir them into the batter. Then make fritters by scooping a generous amount of battered tomatoes at a time and frying on both sides in olive oil on medium heat.

4. Serve hot with yogurt and scrambled eggs. The yogurt makes the difference here.

Note: I love dill, so I use as much as half a cup in this recipe.

Omelet for Summer Lunch

Omeléta me Soutzoúkia

Traditionally prepared with *loukánika*, a variety of garlicky sausage from Tinos, this omelet is a savory Tinos recipe that serves well as lunch. Make it with the sausage of your choice.

Serves 4

1. Wash and peel potatoes and slice in thin rounds. In a frying pan over medium heat, melt the butter, then add the potatoes and the sausage. Shake the pan, cover, lower heat, and cook slowly, stirring frequently, until potatoes are cooked.

2. Beat the eggs, cheese, and milk and pour over the potato mixture. Cook until just set on the bottom, and flip to cook the other side. Do not overcook. Salt and pepper to taste and serve immediately.

4 small potatoes

2 tablespoons butter

2 spicy sausages, sliced

5 eggs

2 tablespoons grated cheese, *myzíthra*, *kasséri*, or feta

2 tablespoons milk

Salt and pepper

Greek Omelet for Two

Oméleta me Tomátes

4 eggs

2 ounces feta

2 scallions, finely cut

2 tablespoons butter

1 large ripe tomato, peeled
and cut up

2 tablespoons snipped
flat-leaf parsley

Pepper

1 teaspoon dried tarragon, or
1 tablespoon fresh

I frequently cooked an omelet for my father when I stayed in Greece during the summers. This version is light, and he enjoyed it for lunch—he never ate anything more than toast for breakfast.

1. Beat the eggs, crumble the feta in them, and set aside. In a frying pan over medium heat, sauté the scallions in the butter, add the chopped tomato, and cook so that some of the liquid evaporates.

2. Pour the egg mixture over the scallions and tomatoes. Sprinkle with parsley, pepper, and tarragon.

3. Cook until the eggs are just set, pulling the edges to let the liquid spill through; flip, finish cooking, and serve. Do not overcook. Slide onto a plate and serve with good bread and a tomato-cucumber salad.

Fresh Green Beans in Sauce

Fasolákia Fréska

For a summer meal, nothing can beat fresh vegetables. This is a recipe that I have taken to so many church suppers that it became well known in my community.

My guests like this one, and my family never tires of it. It was my father-in-law's favorite also; he, like many southerners, called them snap beans. Now that string beans or runner beans, the slender kind, are available year round, I can make this dish at any time. But in the summer when they are fresh, they are a delight to cook and eat. Don't miss them at farmers' markets. When I cook these beans in season, their aroma speaks of summer cooking at home; they are delicious either hot or cold for a summer lunch. They will vary in taste according to the pot you use and the length of time you cook them, so I will reveal here my personal secrets for success.

Serves 10

1 1/2 pounds fresh green beans

1/4 cup best-quality olive oil, or more to taste

1 onion, very finely chopped

2 large ripe tomatoes in season, or 1 14.5-ounce can of peeled tomatoes

1 teaspoon sugar

Salt and pepper to taste

1/4 to 1/2 cup snipped flat-leaf parsley

2 tablespoons snipped dill weed (optional)

1. Prepare the beans by snapping off the stem end; if they are large, remove the strings. Wash in cold running water in a colander. Let them sit on the drain board while you prepare the sauce.

2. In a heavy, three-quart saucepan, heat the olive oil. Sauté the onion until translucent. Add the chopped tomatoes in all their liquid—I mash them so that they resemble a sauce—and the sugar. Bring to a boil and then add all the beans. Stir with a wooden spatula. Add 1/2 cup water, or enough liquid to come halfway up the pot. Add salt and pepper and the herbs. Stir gently. Cover.

3. Bring to a boil again and continue cooking, partially covered, on high heat for 30 minutes. Then check the beans. If they are dry, add a bit of water. In order for the flavor to be intense, I let almost all the liquid evaporate before adding water. Stir once more and let them absorb the sauce. Add half a cup water, cover partially, and simmer for 30 minutes.

4. Test for doneness. If you can cut them with a fork, they are probably ready, but I always taste one to be sure of the texture. (Truly fresh summer beans cook much faster than those bought in other seasons.) The sauce should not be watery—it should be the rich red of the tomatoes and oil.

5. Serve the *fasolákia fréska* with excellent feta—the two flavors blend wonderfully. And don't hesitate to dip your bread into the sauce.

Shrimp with Feta in a Pan

Gharídhes Saganáki

1 pound shrimp

5 scallions, sliced small

1/4 cup olive oil, plus more for finishing

Juice of 1/2 lemon

Salt and pepper

2 fresh tomatoes, peeled and sliced in rounds

1/4 cup snipped flat-leaf parsley

1/2 cup crumbled feta cheese

2 tablespoons dried oregano leaves

1/2 cup bread crumbs

How can we leave summer behind without talking about the gifts of the sea? I lived for quite a few years near the North Carolina coast, and for a while we sailed in the sound and in one of the wide rivers of the state. One day we noticed a shrimp boat just unloading on the river shore. We bought a few pounds and I boiled water in a large pot and dropped the shrimp in it until they turned the unique pink that is all their own. Quickly we spread newspapers and paper towels, peeled the shrimp, and ate them just as they were with the smell of the sea delighting us. They were absolutely delicious. The only thing we added was freshly squeezed lemon juice.

Most of us are not lucky enough to find such fresh shrimp, and transporting them adds to the expense. It is ecologically sound these days to learn to eat frozen shrimp. You may use fresh or frozen shrimp for this dish; the way I cook them still honors their flavors.

Serves 4

1. Bring water to a fast boil and add the shrimp in their shells a few at a time. The moment they start turning color, remove them with a slotted spoon and place them in a bowl. Discard the liquid and peel the shrimp, leaving the tail on if you desire. (This may be done a day in advance.)

2. In an oven-safe frying pan that fits under the broiler, sauté the scallions in 1/4 cup olive oil over a medium flame. Add the shrimp, pour the lemon juice on them, and lightly add salt and pepper. Cover the shrimp with sliced tomatoes, then strew with parsley.

3. Shake the pan and cook quickly, uncovered, over high heat. Remove from heat after liquids evaporate.

4. Just before serving, cover with crumbled or sliced feta cheese, add oregano and bread crumbs, and sprinkle olive oil on top of everything. Pop under the broiler until the feta starts to melt, and serve.

Cold Fish with Mayonnaise

Psári Mayonnaíza

4 pounds cleaned fresh fish (see note)

8 quarts water with 1 table-spoon salt

6 small potatoes

1 medium onion, peeled but whole

6 small carrots, peeled

2 stalks celery with leaves, cut in large pieces

2 sprigs parsley

4 tablespoons olive oil

2 tablespoons lemon juice

1 teaspoon pepper

Salt, to taste

1 cup mayonnaise, preferably homemade (next page)

In my younger years when I lived near the water and had lots of energy, I would give buffet parties at home and invite friends and neighbors who had never been exposed to Greek food, enjoying their reaction. One of my favorite and more spectacular dishes was cold fish with mayonnaise. The best fish for this dish, in season, was sea bass. The yellowtail red snapper, often more readily available, does very well also. But you can use any large fish with white, firm flesh.

Serves 10

1. Rinse the fish in cold water. Place a towel on the cutting board, the fish on it, and with a sharp knife cut each fish in four large segments; set aside.

2. In the 8 quarts salted water, boil the potatoes, onion, carrots, celery, and parsley for about 20 minutes. Now add the fish and cook another 15 minutes or until the fish flesh looks white and opaque. Turn the heat off. With a slotted spoon, very carefully remove the fish and place on a platter. Do the same with the cooked vegetables, making sure the potatoes and carrots are tender; cook longer if they need it. Discard the onion, parsley, and celery. Let everything cool, and save the broth for later or freeze for soup.

3. Peel and discard the skin of the fish, and lift the flesh off the bones. Using your fingers, search the flesh to make sure there are no bones left. Pull the fish into small pieces and toss with the olive oil, lemon juice, and pepper in a large bowl. Taste for seasoning.

4. Peel the potatoes. Keep 1 potato in reserve for decoration and cut the rest into small cubes. Toss the potato cubes with the fish.

5. On an oval platter about 10 inches long (if you have one shaped like a fish, so much the better), pile the fish and potatoes in the shape of a fish's body with head and tail. Spread mayonnaise on top, smoothing it as you go. Now, with slivers of carrots and potato, create any decorations that appeal to you, like fins and large scales. You may also use finely sliced radishes to create a tail, and for the eye and throughout the body I like to use capers.

6. Place toothpicks strategically all over the fish and cover thoroughly with plastic wrap. Do not allow any airholes. Serve later in the day or the next day.

Note: For this recipe, have the fish thoroughly cleaned by your fishmonger, but ask him not to cut off the head or tail.

Homemade Mayonnaise

Makes 1 cup

Put the egg yolks, lemon juice, and sugar in a food processor and process nonstop at medium speed until well blended. Start adding the oil in a steady, thin stream. (If you have a little bottle with an oil spout, this works with precision.) Keep adding the oil until you see that the mayonnaise has thickened. Stop the machine, check the consistency, and at this point add salt and process once more. The mayonnaise will have a creamy or light yellow color. Scoop into a glass container with a lid and refrigerate.

2 yolks from organic eggs

1/4 cup lemon juice

1 teaspoon sugar

1 cup oil of your choice

1 teaspoon salt

Beet and Potato Salad

Rossikí Saláta

This is a very pretty and tasty salad, much more exciting than simple potato salad. You may want to take it to a picnic or a church supper in place of the usual. This dish is especially delicious prepared with homemade mayonnaise (see page 137).

Serves 8–10

1. Boil the beets. If using red beets, peel and wash them under lots of cold water after boiling. Cut them into little cubes and rinse them again. Then wrap them in paper towels. The reason for all this is that red beets bleed into the other vegetables, and you want to reduce that as much as possible.

2. If you are using frozen peas, place them in boiling water, let them reach the boiling point once more, then pour them quickly into a colander to drain; set aside. If using fresh peas, boil them until tender, drain, and cool.

3. Boil the potatoes in their skins with the carrots and eggs in the same large pot, if you like. When hard-boiled, remove eggs with slotted spoon and under running water peel them. Remove carrots and potatoes, and peel.

4. Cut up the cooled potatoes into small cubes and place in large bowl. Cube two of the carrots, reserving one for later, and add to the potatoes. Add the beet cubes and then the cooled peas. Squeeze the juice of half a lemon over everything to keep it vibrant in color. Mix gently with a spatula. Now fold in the mayonnaise and blend together. Add 1 tablespoon capers, two-thirds of the sliced gherkins, the parsley, and salt and pepper to taste. Place in the serving dish. Spread a thin layer of mayonnaise on top, about 2 tablespoons, and decorate with the remaining capers and sliced gherkin, sliced eggs, and long slices of the remaining carrot.

This not only looks pretty, it tastes delicious. If you time it right, I find that this salad is most tasty when just warm, served immediately after preparation, but it is usually served cold as a side dish.

---

2 beets

1 cup peas

4–5 potatoes, enough for 3 cups cooked

3 carrots

2 eggs

Juice of 1/2 lemon

1/2 cup mayonnaise, plus more for topping

2 tablespoons capers, rinsed

3 small sweet gherkins, sliced

1/2 cup chopped parsley

Salt and pepper to taste

Sour Cherry Drink
Vissinádha

Sour cherry syrup (see note)
Cold water

Because of the heat and dryness of the summer, Greeks take advantage of fruits to make delicious drinks. Sour cherries are extremely popular in Greece, not for eating like other fruit, but for imaginative recipes and drinks. My mother, like many other women we knew, made her own liqueur. We watched it happening on our balcony. She would put sour cherries, sugar, and some spices and a bit of brandy in a glass jar, seal it with cork, and leave it in the sun for days.

Serves 1
Place 1/4 inch of syrup in a tall glass and fill with cold water; stir and serve. The syrup is also delicious on vanilla ice cream or yogurt.

Note: The best cherry syrup is found on Greek websites as Sour Cherry Syrup or *Vissinádha* by Kloni.

Fresh Lemonade
Lemonádha

Enough lemons to yield 1 cup lemon juice

1 1/4 cups sugar

2-inch strip of lemon peel

Almost every village garden has a lemon tree, called *lemoniá*. A heartbreakingly beautiful song with words by Elitys calls Greece "land of *lemoniá*, land of joy," so it is natural that we should enjoy the drink as well as all the myriad other uses of its fruit.

Makes enough syrup for 6 glasses
1. Place the lemon juice, sugar, and lemon peel in a small saucepan. Boil, stirring, until the sugar melts. Cool and refrigerate.
2. For each drink, pour 1/4 cup of this syrup into a tall glass, fill with ice water, add a leaf of mint, and serve.

Cool, Creamy, and Fruity Trifle

When I see strawberries and fresh raspberries, my thoughts turn to cool, creamy desserts. The Greeks love ladyfingers, the spongy cookies that absorb creams and flavors. Layer ladyfingers, custard cream, whipping cream, and fresh fruit to make a dessert that's lovely to look at and luscious to eat. I prefer to make my own ladyfingers, since they are rather difficult to find where I live. In Greece you can buy them in any of the sweet shops that adorn each neighborhood, or you may prefer to use slices of sponge cake.

Serves 20

1. Preheat the oven to 300°F.

2. Make the ladyfingers: Beat the yolks in a large bowl with the sugar and extract until light and frothy. In a separate, clean, and cold bowl, whip the egg whites thoroughly. In stages, fold the flour alternately with the whipped whites into the egg yolk mixture; do this gently. Line three baking sheets with parchment or waxed paper. To shape the ladyfingers, use a pastry bag if you have one. I usually dip a tablespoon into the dough and spread it into a 1 x 2-inch rectangle; you may create rectangular or circular shapes. Lay the ladyfingers on the baking sheets, 12 to a sheet. Bake in the preheated oven for about 20 minutes. The ladyfingers will be rosy on the edges; do not bake too long. Remove, slide the parchment paper with the ladyfingers off the pans, cool, then peel the ladyfingers off the paper and store them or use immediately.

3. Make the custard cream: In a 4-quart saucepan, stir together the cold milk, cornstarch, and sugar. Add the lemon peel and vanilla. Over medium heat, stir and cook until mixture thickens and coats a spoon, about 15 minutes. Discard lemon peel.

4. Make the whipped cream: In a cold bowl, combine the cream, sugar, and liqueur and whip with a whisk or handheld electric mixer until firm.

5. To assemble the dessert: In a straight-sided crystal bowl, place in alternating layers one-third of the ladyfingers, custard cream, raspberries or sliced strawberries, and whipped cream. For the third repetition, top the layer of ladyfingers with the two creams and then an artful decoration of the fruit. Cover and refrigerate.

For the ladyfingers:

4 large eggs, separated

1 1/2 cups sugar

1 teaspoon vanilla or brandy extract

2 cups all-purpose flour

For the custard cream:

2 cups whole milk

1/4 cup cornstarch

1/3 cup sugar

1 slice lemon peel

1 teaspoon vanilla extract or a flavor of your choice

For the whipped cream:

8 ounces heavy cream

1 teaspoon sugar

1 teaspoon liqueur of your choice

1 pint strawberries or raspberries

Tart with Cream and Cherries

Toúrta me Kerásia

For the sponge cake:

4 eggs

1 cup sugar

1 cup flour

Pinch of salt

4 tablespoons melted butter

For the syrup:

1 cup sugar

1/4 cup water

2 teaspoons Grand Marnier or, if for children, orange flavoring

For the custard cream:

1/4 cup cornstarch

2 cups whole milk

1/2 cup sugar

2 eggs

1/2 teaspoon vanilla extract

1 cup whipping cream

1 tablespoon sugar

1 cup fresh cherries

The following version is a lighter adaptation of a very rich Greek (Asia Minor) classic.

1. Preheat the oven to 350°F.

2. Make the sponge cake: Beat the eggs and sugar in the mixer until light and frothy. In a separate bowl combine the flour and salt. Now by hand stir flour and melted butter alternately into the egg mixture; do not overmix, because you need it to be light and bubbly. Line a 14 x 11 x 2-inch baking pan with parchment and spread the batter in it; the cake will be rather thin. Bake in the preheated oven for 20 minutes. Set aside to cool.

3. Make a syrup by boiling the sugar and water until the mixture reaches 230°F. Stir in the liqueur. Pour the hot syrup over the cake.

4. Make the custard cream: In a pan that you will use on the range, stir the cornstarch into the cold milk until no lumps remain. In the mixer bowl, beat the sugar with the eggs. Pour this into the milk-cornstarch pan. Place over medium heat, stirring continuously until the mixture thickens and coats a spoon. Remove from heat and add vanilla. Let cool thoroughly.

5. Now beat the whipping cream at high speed. Add the tablespoon of sugar and keep whipping until quite firm. Carefully fold it into the custard, cover, and refrigerate.

6. Cut the cherries in half, removing the pits. Place the cake on a platter. Cover with the custard–whipping cream mixture. Decorate the top with the cherry halves. Cover and refrigerate until ready to serve.

A Menu for Later Summer

Sundried Tomatoes in Batter (*Tomátes Kourkoúti*) 130

Shrimp with Feta in a Pan (*Gharídhes Saganáki*) 134
or Beet and Potato Salad (*Rossikí Saláta*) 139

Fresh Green Beans in Sauce (*Fasolákia Fréska*) 133

Cool, Creamy, and Fruity Trifle 141

Fruit Salad (*Froutosaláta*)

Chickpea Salad (*Revíthia Saláta*)

Grilled Whole Fish (*Psári sti Skhára*)

Fish Salad (*Psarosaláta*)

Lamb Wrapped in Phyllo (*Exohikó*)

Okra in the Fall (*Bámies*)

Zucchini Soufflé (*Kolokythópita*)

Milk Pie (*Ghalatópita*)

Mixed Vegetables (*Briám*)

Spaghetti with Meat Sauce (*Makaróni me Kimá*)

Pasta with Peppers (*Makaróni me Piperiés*)

Triple Moussaka (*Moussakás Triplós*)

Chapter 6

THE PENTECOST SEASON CLOSES: FALL

As August slides into September, the enormous relief of having cooler nights and pleasant days arrives. Greek autumn is not as spectacular as in places of plentiful deciduous trees and cold nights, but it is a lovely time of less humidity, of astonishing colors in the waters of the seas, and, as a dessert of happiness, the incomparable riches of figs and grapes. September is the last month of the Athens-Epidaurus Festival. Music and theater lovers may sit in the open Theater of Herod the Atticus at the foot of the Acropolis or in the beautiful Epidaurus amphitheater, famed for its superb acoustics, to enjoy some of the greatest works of both ancient and modern artists. The big crowds of visiting students have left and life becomes calmer and more introspective as the Greeks prepare their children for a return to school. Fall is also rich in saints' name days.

SAINTS' NAMES AND NATURE'S GIFTS

Name days are all-important to Greek hagiography, church calendar, and culture. Since most Greeks are named after the numerous saints in the Orthodox hagiography, the day on which a certain saint is honored is celebrated like a birthday by the namesake. So even if your friends don't know your birthday, they know your name, and that means that they are free to visit you on that day and to bring you gifts. Every October my native city, Thessaloniki, celebrates the anniversary of St. Demetrius's martyrdom; martyrdom forgotten, they will find this an additional excuse for parties, and all those named Demetris, Demetra, and variations thereof will eat, drink, and dance in ways that would have stunned the original.

There is nothing new in this. Let me go back a few centuries.

The ancient Greeks, with their numerous gods, delighted in honoring them by setting aside a special season in their name. Fortunate for all of us, some of the greatest works of art and of the spirit were created during those sacred days—like the famous Panathenea celebration in honor of Athena, the protector goddess of Athens.

Ancient systems do not die; they merely change names. Modern Greeks do not honor gods; they honor saints. The Greek Orthodox Church has a very heavy saints calendar. Every day of the year has at least one saint appointed to it. The biggies in the fall are Demetrios and Aikaterine (Katherine). Good excuses for baking sweets. So the smart homemaker of old used to be prepared on the name days that related to a member of her family. She would bake in order to be prepared for guests.

In addition to plenty of name days—besides those two, Michalis, Theodoros, Philippos, and Nikolaos come to mind—autumn also offers other priceless gifts of nature. The two fruits I miss the most are grapes from Greek vineyards, sweet with a lovely aroma I have found nowhere else, and figs, large, purple, succulent, and redolent, straight from a fig tree. There was such a tree growing in my grandmother's yard. In a city full of cement and apartment buildings, having a refuge like our grandparents' single home with its own yard and a few plants growing in it was a treat of exotic goodness. There is an aroma emanating from the leaves of a fig tree, but I have noticed it only in dry lands. You may replicate it if you rub a bit of the rough leaf between your fingers.

In Mediterranean lands, in dry seasons, when the wind is causing a seductive incense to float toward you as you walk, and you find yourself almost at the point of sweet inebriation of the best kind, look around you and you will discover a fig tree. August and September are the months of ripeness for both figs and grapes, but it has been a long time since I happened to be in Greece during those months. So I live with longing. To ease it, I order dried Greek figs from Kalamata through the wonder that is now the Internet, but nothing replaces the rich seed-filled succulence of fresh figs. And I always miss the grapes. If you have a chance to go to Greece in early fall, do so and ask for fruit.

Fruit Salad

Froutosaláta

1 melon, cantaloupe or honeydew

10 fresh figs, if available

60 grapes, green and red

2 bananas

1 large apple

1 orange

10 large strawberries

Juice of 1 lemon

1 kiwi fruit

1 star fruit (optional)

1 cup roasted and peeled pistachio nuts

How can we capture some of the blessings of Greek autumn in our kitchens? Together with the two wondrous fruits, we have an abundance of zucchini, tomatoes, okra, potatoes, and, from the island of Aegina, superb pistachio nuts. It is rare for Greeks to use fruit in recipes—they eat it raw, or they preserve it as spoon sweets and as glazed fruit. However, they are beginning to experiment with new salads, and I do love a fruit salad. This is my version.

Serves 10

1. Cut up the fruits thus: the peeled melon in bite-size pieces, figs in quarters, large grapes in half, peeled bananas in rounds, the apple in very slender wedges, the orange in segments without membranes, strawberries sliced so the red shows. Reserve kiwi and star fruit for the top.

2. Mix sliced fruits gently together. Immediately squeeze lemon juice over them: this keeps them from discoloring and brings out their sweetness. Arrange some of each fruit in individual serving dishes so that it looks colorful and attractive. Decorate with sliced kiwi and star fruit and scatter pistachios on top.

Whipped cream is the richer dressing for this salad. But plain Greek yogurt stirred with a teaspoon of sugar in a small cup next to the fruit is also delicious.

Chickpea Salad

Revíthia Saláta

One of the hardest legumes to cook to an edible tenderness is the chickpea; it takes hours of boiling. But take heart: there are excellent canned chickpeas, known also as garbanzo beans. This is one of the few exceptions to my efforts never to use canned vegetables—the others being artichoke hearts and tomato products. But I make sure to rinse the chickpeas thoroughly under cold running water so that the salt in the can disappears.

This salad may serve as a starter or as a main dish for a light lunch.

Serves 8

1. Place the chickpeas in a bowl and mix in the scallions, salt and pepper, celery, and parsley leaves. On the top arrange the feta, cucumber, grapes, and pitted olives.

2. Whip together the olive oil and lemon juice with a bit of mint or basil (you may substitute vinegar for the lemon if you like; you may also use mayonnaise in your dressing). Pour gently so that the dressing coats everything.

3. Cover the salad and let it absorb the flavors. Wash and dry the leaves of romaine lettuce and use each as a little serving "boat" in which you place a scoop of the chickpea salad.

2 cans chickpeas, well rinsed

4 scallions, cut in slender rings

Salt and pepper

1 stalk celery, chopped

1/2 cup flat-leaf parsley leaves

1/2 cup crumbled feta

1 cucumber, peeled and cut in cubes

1 cup seedless white grapes

8 pitted Kalamata olives

1/2 cup olive oil

1/4 cup lemon juice

Mint or basil leaves

Romaine lettuce leaves

Grilled Whole Fish

Psári sti Skhára

Greeks have eaten fish for millennia. They tend toward simplicity rather than elaboration in the cooking of seafood because they honor the taste and smell of the sea and don't want to cover it up. One year when we were young parents and our children were still more interested in playing together than in sightseeing, we went to the island of Kos and spent a few days roughing it. My relatives were embarrassed, but my American husband considers it the best vacation of his life. We drank our coffee under a vine in a poor man's yard and ate bread, cheese, and fruit and felt like rich diners. At the shore we bought *barbounia*, red mullet, the fish most beloved by Greeks, from someone who had just caught them, and the owner of the taverna grilled them for us over a fire on the sand while the water lapped at our feet. All we added was olive oil and lemon juice. In its simplicity it was the highest culinary experience. Years later my husband still talks about it with pleasure.

In good weather, the best way is to grill the fish over charcoal. In the winter, bake it inside. On both occasions leave it whole.

Serves 4

1. Preheat oven to 450°F, or prepare outdoor grill.

2. After cleaning them, wash the fish thoroughly and dry with paper towels. In a 14 x 9 x 2-inch baking pan place 2 tablespoons olive oil and rub both sides of the fish in it so they are well coated. Score them on top with two large gashes to the spine. Inside the body cavities stuff onion and lemon slices, and pour lemon juice over the fish. Sprinkle with salt, pepper, and oregano. Add 1/4 cup water to the pan and bake in the preheated oven for 15 minutes. The fish is done when the flesh is white and opaque close to the spine.

3. For outside grilling, prepare it the same way but without the cavity stuffing: oil it well and, while grilling, baste it with *ladholémono*— oil and lemon juice whipped together.

4. Serve the fish with slices of tomatoes and cucumbers, parsley, and fresh scallions also doused with *ladholémono*.

5. If you have leftovers, make a salad; few meals are more delicious for lunch.

2 1-pound whole trout, snapper, or any good fish in season

2 tablespoons olive oil, plus more for *ladholémono*

1 onion, sliced

2 lemons, sliced

Juice of 1 or 2 lemons

1 teaspoon salt

1 teaspoon ground pepper

1 tablespoon Greek oregano

2 ripe tomatoes

2 cucumbers

1/4 cup chopped parsley

4 scallions

Fish Salad

Psarosaláta

2 cups cooked fish with white, lean flesh

2 scallions

1/2 cup snipped flat-leaf parsley

1/2 cup olive oil

Juice of 1 lemon

Salt and pepper

Leaves of 1 romaine lettuce heart

2 ripe tomatoes

2 cucumbers

This dish is great for leftover baked, boiled, fried, or grilled fish. I love having leftovers after cooking fish. One of the most delicious memories from my mother's table offerings is this.

Serves 4

Remove all skin and bones from the fish. Pull the fish flesh with your fingers and pile it in a shallow bowl. Mix it with finely sliced scallions and snipped parsley. Pour on the olive oil and lemon juice to taste and season with salt and pepper. Toss to coat the fish. Place the lettuce leaves on a serving platter and mound the fish salad on them. Surround the salad with sliced tomatoes and cucumbers and enjoy!

TOURING AND EATING IN GREECE IN THE FALL

Thinking of fall brings to mind a tour I led to Greek historic sites with about thirty North Carolinians over three weeks of a lovely October. To go on a tour of Greece means going on an eating adventure. But perhaps more fun than eating for me was watching my friends try pronouncing the various names and recipes; I spent quite a bit of time coaching them as they tried to remember these unusual words for their next attempt at ordering.

While I have sometimes criticized both Greeks and Americans on many different issues, I am also quick to praise them when the occasion arises. If I were to choose my favorite tourists, I would choose Americans, despite the myths told about them. The Americans I have led on Greek tours have been the most agreeable, the best mannered, and the most appreciative of tourists. This is not my opinion only; it is the consensus of the Greeks who deal with tourists from around the world. They may be the easiest to please because they are not afraid to try different and new things both as activities and as culinary experiences. It is amusing for Greeks to hear them ask, "What is this called?" Regardless of the answer, the next time they will not be able to repeat it. Greek is not an easy language for Americans to pronounce. But if one makes the effort, the Greek chef or waiter will be delighted.

For many Americans traveling Greece, lamb is a new experience since beef is so much more plentiful and popular in the United States. As our "eating tour" of Greece continued, my American friends were not disappointed in the lamb dishes they tried. The old National Road that connected Athens to Thessaloniki passes through some stunning countryside. Near Athens it rolls by the sea. Nearer Thessaloniki it passes under the shadow of Mt. Olympus and then climbs above the blue and brilliant Aegean. Our tour stopped at a solitary restaurant near Larissa for a quick meal. It was not intended to be anything spectacular, but in fact the dishes were delicious. After a marvelous meal I went to the kitchen to congratulate and talk to the chef, Demetrios. The lamb dish called *exohikó* (next page) is what he served us that day.

Lamb Wrapped in Phyllo

Exohikó

1 leek and 6 scallions

12 ounces (1 1/2 sticks) butter, divided

2 pounds lean lamb, cut into 1/4-inch cubes

1 cup chopped onion

Freshly ground pepper

1 teaspoon salt

1 pound phyllo

1/4 pound *kasséri*, sliced thinly (if unavailable, use aged Provolone)

4 hard-boiled eggs, sliced

This recipe comes courtesy of Chef Demetrios. His lamb dish is a crusty thick cylinder of phyllo pastry, filled with succulent lamb, vegetables, and cheeses. The chef calls it *exohikó*, which means "of the countryside," but it looks good enough to be served on an elegant buffet table. There are other recipes with the same name, wrapped in grape leaves or paper, but this particular *exohikó* is a winner.

Note: Before working with phyllo, please see advice on its handling, page 14.

Serves 6

1. Wash and prep the leek (see page 54). Cut leek and scallions into 1/2-inch-long pieces and set aside. In a large, heavy pan over high heat, melt half a stick of butter, then brown the meat cubes in two batches. With a slotted spoon, remove them and place them inside a bowl. In the same pan, sauté the onion, scallions, and leek until almost translucent. Return the meat and all its juices to the pan, add 1/2 cup water, scrape the bottom, cover the pan, and cook the meat and vegetables over low heat for 30 minutes. Checking for tenderness, uncover and let the liquids evaporate, cooking 10 more minutes. Turn the heat off, grind pepper over the meat, sprinkle with salt, stir, and let cool.

2. Preheat the oven to 425°F.

3. Prepare your work surface for the phyllo. Have ready 1 stick melted butter, a pastry brush, the sliced *kasséri*, the cooled meat mixture, and the sliced eggs.

4. Working with three sheets of phyllo at a time, butter each sheet with quick wide strokes and stack them, the narrow end toward you. Leaving 2-inch margins on bottom and sides, spread with 2 tablespoonfuls of the meat mixture; cover with egg and 1 *kasséri* slice. Don't neglect to scoop up the delicious onion sauce with the meat. Fold the bottom edge over the meat, then each of the long sides to meet in the middle. Now butter this surface, and roll the meat away from you. You will create a 4 x 1-inch cylinder with the filling nicely contained. Brush the edges with butter and seal. Place in a 2-inch-deep metal baking pan. Repeat until meat mixture is used up.

5. Brush tops lightly with butter so they will turn golden. Bake in the preheated oven for 15 minutes. (You may freeze the portions you are not ready to bake until you have company.) Serve hot.

Variation: Try this recipe with beef, pork, or chicken. You may also use spinach instead of leeks. For the cheese, stay with *kasséri*, which melts beautifully, or if unavailable, with Provolone.

Okra in the Fall

Bámies

Select the smallest okra in the bin; they cook and taste the best.

Serves 6–8

1 pound small okra

Vinegar for sprinkling

1/2 cup excellent olive oil

1 onion, sliced into slender rounds

2 large ripe tomatoes, peeled and sliced into rounds

1/2 cup snipped flat-leaf parsley

1 teaspoon sugar

Salt and pepper

Juice of 1 lemon

1. Wash the okra under cold water and dry thoroughly in a towel. You will need a small knife with a very sharp blade. Take each pod and peel carefully and gently around the woody head, taking care not to pierce the flesh. This will take a bit of time, but if you sit out-doors, you will enjoy doing it. Spread the okra on a cookie sheet, sprinkle with vinegar, and leave out in the sunlight to dry.

2. In a frying pan, heat the olive oil and brown the okra quickly and lightly. Immediately cover them with the onions, tomatoes, and parsley. Sprinkle with the sugar, salt, and pepper, then douse with lemon juice. Cover and shake the pan gently.

3. Simmer the okra so all these delicious flavors blend together. When most of the liquid has evaporated and you are left with a rich sauce, taste one of the okra. It doesn't take long for them to cook, about 30 minutes if they are small and fresh. They are good both hot and cold.

Zucchini Soufflé

Kolokythópita

For the filling:

3 cups grated zucchini

1 teaspoon salt

2 scallions

3 tablespoons snipped fresh dill

4 leaves mint or basil

3 eggs, slightly beaten

1/2 cup heavy cream

1 cup grated Parmesan

1 cup crumbled feta

1 teaspoon freshly ground pepper

10 sheets (1/4 pound) phyllo

4–5 tablespoons olive oil

Zucchini, the humble vegetable that never ceases its generous giving, finds honor and glamour in this recipe that comes courtesy of my friend Eleni Melyrritou, who lives in Nashville and Greece. This is good enough for both family and the most sophisticated company.

Note: Before working with phyllo, please see advice on its handling, page 14.

Yields 8 pie-size slices

1. After you grate the zucchini, place it and the salt in a colander for 1 hour to draw and drain its liquids. To make sure that not much liquid remains, roll the zucchini in a clean towel and squeeze before use. Mix gently but thoroughly with the remaining filling ingredients just before assembling. (It's important to do this just before baking; you don't want the mixture to sit and create excess liquids.)

2. You may use a deep quiche pan or, my preference, a 10-inch springform pan. With a springform you can open the sides and the tart remains on the rimless bottom, so you can slide it off on a cutting board—much easier to serve in wedges. Make sure you grease all surfaces well.

3. Preheat the oven to 350°F.

4. Take one phyllo sheet at a time, brush with the olive oil, and place in the pan with one end flat on the bottom and the other climbing up a side and overhanging. Make absolutely sure that you brush the edges well; if the phyllo is not well oiled, the overhang will dry and crumble. After you place each sheet, rotate the pan about 36 degrees (one-tenth) to receive the next sheet, so all the surface is covered; this will give you a good bottom and side crust.

5. Pour the filling into the phyllo, then bring the edges over it, extending about an inch toward the center, and tuck the phyllo overhang into the filling, leaving a narrow rim. Bake in the preheated oven for 50 minutes. Gently insert a toothpick, taking care not to make the soufflé fall. If it comes out clean, it's ready.

6. Let the pie sit for 10 minutes before releasing the spring and sliding it off to a cutting board; cut in wedges and serve to the praise of your guests. This is rich, so one wedge makes a generous serving.

Milk Pie

Ghalatópita

This is a spectacular dessert for a family gathering or guests (with thanks to my niece Natassa).

Serves 12

1. Preheat the oven to 400°F.

2. Combine all filling ingredients in a saucepan and cook slowly over medium heat until the mixture begins to thicken. Do not let it reach custard stage. Remove from heat to cool.

3. Butter a 14 x 11 x 2-inch metal pan. (Or, if you have a pretty pottery pan, use it and serve the *ghalatópita* directly from it.)

4. Take a sheet of phyllo, butter it, and place lengthwise in the pan so it hangs over one side. Sprinkle with 2 tablespoons ground almonds, cinnamon, and 1 tablespoon sugar. Repeat with three more phyllo sheets, staggering them so that the pan bottom is covered and the phyllo hangs over the 4 sides. Place an additional phyllo sheet on the bottom of the pan. Now pour the filling inside the pan, tuck the phyllo in over the edges, brush the phyllo edges with butter, and bake for 20 minutes. Remove and sprinkle with cinnamon.

For the filling:

4 cups whole milk

1/2 cup fine semolina flour

1/2 cup sugar

1 teaspoon vanilla or almond extract

2 eggs, beaten

For the pie assembly:

4 tablespoons melted butter

5 sheets phyllo

1/2 cup ground almonds

Cinnamon for sprinkling, about 1 teaspoon

4 tablespoons sugar

Mixed Vegetables

Briám

3/4 cup olive oil

2–3 large potatoes (about 1 pound total)

4 tomatoes

1 red onion

2 1/2-pound eggplants

3 zucchini (about 1 pound total)

2 peppers, green and red

2 tablespoons oregano

1 tablespoon sea salt

1 tablespoon freshly ground pepper

1 lemon

This is such a wonderful way to enjoy vegetables in season. A few years ago, when I was in Várkiza, a suburb of Athens on the sea, where my sister lives, a neighbor arrived with a pan filled with colorful vegetables. He had heard that I was interested in writing about food, and he brought me his favorite dish. In Greece, except in restaurant kitchens, it is rare to meet a man who will admit interest in cooking, so I paid attention to our visitor. I remember vividly the appearance of that dish. So now, when I prepare *briám*, I pause to admire the layers of vegetables before I put them in the oven. They look marvelous beforehand and they taste delicious afterwards. Several of the senses are satisfied, and that's what food offers us in abundance.

Serves 10

1. Preheat the oven to 400°F.

2. Pour half of the oil to cover the bottom of an 18 x 12-inch baking pan.

3. Peel the potatoes, tomatoes, and onion and slice in slender rounds. Wash the remaining vegetables. Trim and slice the eggplant and zucchini crosswise in 1/4-inch rounds, and the peppers in thinner rings.

4. Layer the sliced potatoes on the bottom of the pan, followed by the eggplant and then the zucchini. Now intersperse the red onion and pepper rings to form a colorful top layer, and scatter the tomato slices so all the colors show. Sprinkle with oregano, salt, pepper, and the remaining oil. Bake, uncovered, in the preheated oven until the tomatoes turn color, about 40 minutes. Squeeze lemon juice over everything (optional) and serve with generous slices of feta and crusty bread.

❧ Saints and National Remembrance ❧

Having lived in the United States for decades, I get amused whenever I consider my native land's inextricable links between church and state. As I am writing this, celebrations are taking place all over Greece commemorating Greek Orthodoxy and Hellenism—the national identity of the Greeks. Even though most Greeks are thoroughly secular, they honor their religious rituals and traditions and they consider the heritage of Orthodoxy as their national identity also. Rituals, especially those connected with eating together, have a cohesive effect on a homogenous society, and Greek culture has benefited from this cohesiveness.

On September 14 the country celebrates the great religious holiday of the Elevation or Exaltations of the Holy Cross, but very few seem aware of its profound religious significance. It's a bit strange to think of the Crucifixion while feasting, but, for the Greeks, the Cross is tied more to their love of Helena, the mother of Constantine the Great, than to that horrible death on Golgotha.

The story goes like this: Helena was the mother of the fourth-century emperor who moved the capital from Rome to Byzantium/Constantinople and proclaimed Christianity legal and even mandatory. She was a devout woman who visited Jerusalem in order to find the "holy places"; in the course of her efforts she claimed to have found the genuine cross of Golgotha—reminiscent of the search for the Holy Grail in legends from other parts of Europe. Without expressing any doubt, every Greek Orthodox religious writer I have read claims that Helena was successful in her search. These stories seem to be like a glue that binds the whole religious/ethnic identity together.

In the Greek countryside, a communal celebration is call *panegýri*, a word recognized by those who studied the classics and the panegyrics written by great orators or poets in praise of a hero. With a prefix like *pan-*, you recognize also that this refers to the gathering of many or all people. So it's a wonderful word for a celebratory gathering. The newer word, much used, like the English "party," is *ghléndi*. Both mean having fun, the kind that always involves eating, drinking, and dancing (those lovely communal Greek folk dances).

What bemuses me is the juxtaposition, the irony hidden in the announcement that translates thus: "After partying all night, the faithful walk to the church for the elevation of the Holy Cross, and then they return to the square to continue the *ghléndi*." I find something quintessentially Greek in this commemoration of one of the most horrific events in history with the partying before and after. Of interest to us here is that it is centered around eating together.

Another cause for both religious and national *panegýri* is the day of St. Demetrius, the particular saint loved by the people of my hometown, Thessaloniki. In fact, I was born and raised just a street away from the great Byzantine church of Ayios Demetrios in the city, proclaimed a UNESCO site in the seventies.

St. Demetrius's Day arrives just two days before the second greatest national day (the first being March 25); this one is the commemoration of Greek resistance to Fascist Italy in 1940. In the dark of night, at three a.m. before the dawn of October 28, the Italian ambassador brought an ultimatum from Mussolini to Prime Minister Metaxas of Greece demanding free passage through Greece, which would result in the occupation of the country by the Italians. Metaxas answered him with a resounding *No!* (*OXI!* or *okhi!*) in Greek, thus ushering Greece into World War II. This is known as OXI day. The reason this is such a significant commemoration of great national pride is that little Greece, quite poor at that time, defeated Mussolini's well-equipped army in the ferocious mountains of Albania— the first defeat of Fascism by a free country in that terrible war. So on that day, October 28, all of Greece celebrates.

Since Greeks and Italians resumed their friendly relations after the war, I thought this commemoration would be the perfect occasion for talking about pasta and how the Greeks cook and eat it.

Spaghetti with Meat Sauce

Makaróni me Kimá

Makaróni—the general term for pasta—is sold in Greece by numbers that refer to the thickness of the strands. The thinnest used is spaghetti-size; the thickest is the macaroni used for pastitsio, a popular recipe that tourists get tired of. Before television and its ubiquitous cooking programs, Greeks had specific and limited ways with pasta—at least in our home. This was one we never got tired of.

2 pounds ground beef

1 large onion, chopped fine

2 tablespoons butter, for browning meat (optional)

1/2 cup red wine

1/2 6-ounce can tomato paste, diluted in 1 cup warm water

1 14.5-ounce can whole tomatoes, or fresh when in season

1 cinnamon stick (optional)

Sea salt

Freshly ground pepper

1/4 cup snipped flat-leaf parsley

2 tablespoons oregano

2 pounds spaghetti

4 tablespoons butter, or more to taste

Sharp cheese for grating

Serves 8

1. Brown the meat and onions in a heavy, wide pan. (You may add 2 tablespoons butter if you like, but you can also brown it dry.) When the meat turns brown, pour the wine over it and stir. Then add the diluted tomato paste, followed by the tomatoes, which you have mashed. Stir well. Add the cinnamon stick, if using. Season with salt, pepper, parsley, and oregano. Cook until the liquids are reduced and the meat is cushioned in a rich and redolent red sauce. Remove the cinnamon stick if you used it.

2. Boil the pasta according to the package directions. Drain but do not rinse. In the same pot, melt 4 tablespoons butter until it almost browns. Pour the pasta back into the pot and stir quickly so that it is well coated with butter.

3. Serve the pasta in deep dishes. Ladle sauce over the pasta and serve freshly grated sharp cheese with it. We like grated *kefalotýri*.

Variations: You may also serve the spaghetti with just tomato sauce or plain, buttered as above, with crumbled feta cheese, which is the way we liked it at home.

Pasta with Peppers

Makaróni me Piperiés

Any kind of pasta would work here, not just spaghetti.

Serves 6

1. Wash peppers and slice in strips. Sauté the onion and garlic in half the oil and then stir in the peppers and cook, covered, over low heat until they soften, about 1 hour. Check periodically to be sure they don't burn. If you need to add liquid, add 1/2 cup red wine. Add the parsley and remove from heat.

2. Cook the pasta according to package directions, then drain. Pour 1/4 cup olive oil in the pot and turn the heat to high. Stir the drained pasta into the pot, turn it quickly with a wooden spoon, and then place in a large serving bowl. Pour the cooked vegetables over the spaghetti and serve immediately with the cheese of your choice. With peppers I prefer the taste of feta or *myzíthra*.

4 bell peppers, green, orange, red, and yellow

1 onion, chopped

2 peeled garlic cloves

1/2 cup olive oil

1/2 cup red wine (optional)

1/4 cup snipped flat-leaf parsley

1 pound spaghetti

Triple Moussaka

Moussakás Triplós

For the meat sauce:

4 tablespoons olive oil

2 pounds ground meat of
your choice

2 onions, chopped fine

3 garlic cloves, chopped fine

1 14.5-ounce can tomatoes

1 6-ounce can tomato paste,
diluted with 2 cups water

1 teaspoon salt

1 teaspoon pepper

2 tablespoons oregano

1 bay leaf

4 large potatoes (2 pounds
total)

1/4 cup butter

5–6 zucchini (2 pounds total)

6 small eggplant, or 2 large
(2 pounds total)

Sea salt

2 recipes béchamel (page 92)

1/2 cup grated sharp cheese

At this stage, most Greek cookbooks would include pastitsio, but it has become such a cliché that I will avoid it. Instead, I offer another version of moussaka, this one from my sister Niki.

As I said before, the women in my family are excellent cooks, and they are very careful about the traditional overconsumption of olive oil and fried foods. Both my sisters have devoted their whole lives to their families, and for me they stand as the quintessential Greek *noikokyrás*—the women who rule their households with care and beauty. With a very serious nod to healthy eating, they have reduced the amount of fat in recipes and the consumption of meats. The old-fashioned moussaka used to contain so much fat that we cooked it on very special occasions only. Now my sister Niki tells me that she makes a moussaka that utilizes four vegetables, and only one of them is lightly fried. Here is her version of a complete meal in a casserole for a large family gathering. It is delicious, and guests at my table have enjoyed it fully.

Serves 12

1. In a saucepan over medium heat, heat the olive oil, then brown the meat, onions, and garlic; add the tomatoes and diluted tomato paste and bring to a boil. Add the salt and pepper and herbs, stir, then lower heat and simmer uncovered while you prepare vegetables. Add more water as needed so meat sauce doesn't dry out.

2. Meanwhile, peel the potatoes and slice into very slender rounds. Melt the butter in a wide pan over high heat and add the potatoes. When the bottom layer starts turning crisp, flip with spatula, turn heat to low, cover, and let the potatoes cook more slowly. Meanwhile, prepare the rest of the vegetables. Wash the zucchini and slice in slender circles. Cut off the stems of the eggplant, cut off alternating strips of the skin, and then slice them crosswise into rounds less than 1/4 inch thick. Salt zucchini and eggplant generously with sea salt and place in a colander to drain them of liquids. Then rinse and wrap in clean tea towels until ready to use.

3. Remove the bay leaf from the sauce and discard. Preheat the oven to 350°F.

4. Prepare the béchamel as directed for *moussaká papoutsákia* (page 92). It should be thick but spreadable.

5. Arrange the potatoes as a bottom layer in a large, buttered baking dish (I use my 14 x 11 x 2-inch CorningWare). Spread one-third of the meat sauce over the potatoes, then add the sliced zucchini. Spread another third of the meat sauce on top of the zucchini, followed by the eggplant. Add the rest of the meat sauce, spreading it evenly. Spread béchamel sauce on the moussaka. Sprinkle grated cheese on top.

6. Bake covered for 45 minutes, then uncovered for 15 minutes. Serve hot.

A Menu for Fall

Fruit Salad (*Froutosaláta*) 148

Triple Moussaka (*Moussakás Triplós*) 164

Okra in the Fall (*Bámies*) 155

A Menu for a Birthday or Name Day

Chickpea Salad (*Revíthia Saláta*) 149

Lamb Wrapped in Phyllo (*Exohikó*) 154 *or*
(vegetarian) Zucchini Soufflé (*Kolokythópita*) 156

Fish Salad (*Psarosaláta*) 152

Milk Pie (*Ghalatópita*) 157

Winter Salad (*Himoniátike Saláta*)

Stuffed Cabbage Leaves (*Lahanodolmádhes*)

Pork with Celery (*Hirinó me Sélino*)

Meat and Rice Balls in Avgolémono (*Yiouvarlákia*)

Tart with Peppers and Mushrooms
(*Toúrta me Piperiés kai Manitária*)

Rice with Dates (*Rízi me Hourmádhes*)

Yogurt Cake (*Hálsema*)

Copenhagen Pastry in Honor of a King (*Copenhághê*)

Christmas Cookies in Honey (*Melomakárona*)

Shortbread Cookies (*Kourabiédhes*)

Chestnut Truffles (*Kástana Troúfes*)

New Year's Bread (*Vasilópita*)

Bean Soup (*Fasoládha*)

Chicken Soup (*Kotósoupa*)

Chicken with Retsina Wine (*Methysméno Kotópoulo*)

Chicken Roasted with Orzo (*Kóta me Piláfi*)

Rice Pudding (*Rizógalo*)

Potatoes with Sauce (*Patátes Yiahní*)

Chapter 7

ADVENT

Advent is not observed among the Orthodox as it is in the Western Church. For Western liturgical churches—Roman Catholic, Anglican, and Lutheran—Advent starts with the fourth Sunday before Christmas. This falls either on the last Sunday of November, or the first Sunday in December. For the Orthodox Church, Advent starts on November 15, following St. Philip's Day. In older, more religiously observant days, this was also a season of fast. Still, Advent and Christmas never reached the importance of the Lenten and Paschal seasons in Greece. Most of the customs observed today, especially in urban settings, remind one of northern European lands and of the influence American culture has had on the rest of the world. The decorations, Santa Claus, and the sounds of carols strike a discordant note in the Greek environment.

Comfort Food and Seasonal Joy

In leaner times, Greek women brought forth their most successful culinary and, especially, baking gifts during this season. To those of us who honor the particularities of cultural differences, the loss of diversity that has resulted from the ubiquitous presence of television and the youth cult of America that has now permeated world cultures is a cause for regret and even for mourning what is past. It is mostly in villages and islands that Greeks still preserve some of the customs of old. It is delightful to search and find the individual traditions of each island.

One common culinary characteristic emerges for the season: the meat of choice for Advent and Christmas is pork. The family pig is fed and cared for from October on, to be eaten during the feast days of Christmas. The stuffing, roasting, and eating of turkey is undoubtedly an American tradition that has infiltrated the holidays in places where turkey was not eaten in years past. On several islands the preparation for slaughtering the pig reminds me of the customs of farming communities in eastern North Carolina, my erstwhile home. One year I was invited to view a hog killing or pig pickin'. All the neighbors gathered in the yard or the house, and every part of the pig was utilized in the pickin' process. In the middle of the day, the women laid tables with all kinds of dishes brought from their homes, and the hosts and their neighbors took a break to eat before returning to the yard to make sausage and to cut pork chops, hams, and bacon.

So it was with the Greek countryside around Christmastime. No one was left to go hungry; those who had shared with those who had not. In the places of my family heritage, Epirus in the west and Thrace in the northeast, pork meat was usually accompanied by cabbage. It is said that meat wrapped in cabbage leaves (see *lahanodolmádhes*, page 171) started in the days of Byzantium and that it was symbolic of the Christ Child wrapped in swaddling clothes. Other food symbolism extends to:

Honey, which represents every family member's contribution to the household's coffers;

Wine, which represents the wish for family members to grow strong like grapevines;

Pitas, which express hope for the abundance of wheat; and

Apples, which are symbolic of good health, and express the wish for everyone in the family to have the rosy color of health, like the red of an apple.

One reminder that Christmas celebration has been influenced by the north is the detail that, for a long time in this season, Greeks decorated ship replicas instead of the Christmas tree—proof of their long existence as a seafaring nation. As far as I can determine, the one island observing this ancient custom today is Chios. The rest have replaced their ship replicas with Christmas trees.

Winter Salad

Himoniátike Saláta

3 carrots

1/2 cup golden raisins

1/2 cup toasted walnuts or almonds

2 cups baby spinach and radicchio, mixed

2 oranges

1 large apple

1 banana

1 pear

1/2 cup currants

For the dressing:

1/3 cup oil

4 tablespoons balsamic vinegar

1/4 cup sweet wine, Mavrodaphne (see note) or port

This is a good time to utilize the riches of the season in the making of salads.

Serves 6

1. Shave the carrots into ribbons with a potato peeler and place in a bowl. Toss them with the raisins and nuts.

2. Cut the stems from the spinach and radicchio. Add their leaves to the salad for color. Separate the oranges into segments and remove the skins. Arrange in overlapping layers over the spinach. Do the same with the apple, banana, and pear so that you have a pretty design of overlapping slices and colors on top. Sprinkle currants over everything.

3. Combine the dressing ingredients and pour all over the salad. Serve.

Note: Mavrodaphne is a dark red, very sweet, aromatic Greek wine.

Stuffed Cabbage Leaves

Lahanodolmádhes

This dish is a must for Christmas Day in many parts of the land.

Makes 20 *dolmádhes*

1. In the oil or butter, brown the pork in a heavy pan together with the scallions and onion. Add the rice and stir thoroughly. Add the broth, herbs, and salt and pepper. Bring to a boil, then lower to simmer until rice is almost cooked, about 30 minutes. Turn the heat off and let the filling cool.

2. In a large pot, bring 8 quarts of water to a boil. Remove 2–3 outer leaves of the cabbage and reserve. Rinse the head of cabbage, cut around the hard core with a knife, remove the core, and discard it. With the stem side facing down, lower cabbage into the pot and boil for 15 minutes. Set a colander in the sink, very carefully remove the cabbage from the hot water, place it stem side up in the colander, and run lots of cold water over it. Gently separate the cabbage leaves; lay them out on a large platter.

3. Whip the egg and stir it into the cooled meat-rice filling. Place the reserved outer leaves on the bottom of a Dutch oven or a large frying pan with a lid. These extra leaves will protect the *dolmádhes* from scorching.

4. Now form the *dolmádhes*: With kitchen scissors trim the hard ribs of the cabbage leaves so that they are soft and pliable. Place each leaf in turn on a plate, scoop a heaping tablespoon of filling on its edge, and roll up like a cigar, folding first the bottom and then the two sides over the filling. The rolls will be about 2 1/2 inches long.

5. Place them seam down and side by side in tight rows in the pan lined with outer leaves. Pour over them butter, lemon juice, and water to cover; weigh down with an inverted plate.

6. Bring to a boil, lower to simmer, and cook for about 1 hour, adding water as needed. They should be left with a cup of broth.

7. For *avgolémono*: Dissolve cornstarch in 1 cup cold water. Whip the egg yolks in bowl, add the lemon juice, then cornstarch and water. Ladle hot broth into egg mixture. Pour *avgolémono* over *dolmádhes*; shake pan and serve immediately.

For the filling:

2 tablespoons olive oil or butter

1 pound lean ground pork

3 scallions, white with about an inch of the dark green, sliced fine

1 medium onion, chopped fine

1/2 cup uncooked rice

2 cups low-sodium chicken broth

1/2 cup mixed and snipped fresh parsley and dill

Salt and pepper to taste

1 egg

1 large green cabbage

4 tablespoons melted butter

Juice of 1/2 lemon, strained

For the *avgolémono* sauce:

1 tablespoon cornstarch

2 egg yolks

Juice of 1 lemon

Pork with Celery

Hirinó me Sélino

3 pounds lean pork shoulder, cut in small cubes

6 stalks celery from the heart, cut in 2-inch pieces, plus some leaves

1 leek, white part only, chopped

1/2 stick butter

1 onion, chopped

2 tablespoons flour

1 cup chicken broth or stock

Freshly ground pepper, to taste

For the *avgolémono* sauce:

2–3 large egg yolks

1/4 cup lemon juice

1 tablespoon cornstarch

Since the meat traditionally eaten during rural Greek winters is pork, this recipe is appropriate for cold weather. It is also a delicious way to cook pork—my favorite way, actually.

Serves 8

1. Blanch the pork pieces for 3 minutes. Drain and set aside.

2. Blanch the celery and leek for 3 minutes, cool under running water, drain, and set aside.

3. In the butter, in a heavy casserole, sauté the onion, then add the pork pieces and brown well. Sprinkle them with flour and stir gently. Add the chicken broth or stock, bring to a boil, immediately turn to simmer, and cook for 30 minutes. At this point add the celery and leeks with 1 cup warm water or additional stock, cover, and simmer until the celery is tender, about 1 hour. Test meat and celery for doneness. Remove them to a hot serving dish and keep warm.

4. Keep the cooking liquid hot but not boiling. There should be at least one cup; add water if necessary.

5. Prepare the *avgolémono* sauce: Whip the yolks in a deep bowl, then add the lemon juice very slowly, whipping all the time. Stir in the cornstarch. Still whipping and very gradually, add cooking liquid to the egg mixture until you have a thick, rich sauce. Pour the sauce all over the meat and celery and stir gently. Grind some fresh pepper on it and serve over rice or pasta. Dry white wine, a baguette, and a green salad complete this main course.

Meat and Rice Balls in Avgolémono

Yiouvarlákia

This delicious winter soup, a favorite of my husband's, is very similar to the filling for the rolled cabbage leaves.

Serves 4

1. Mix the meat, onion, rice, parsley, egg, and salt and pepper to taste. Dipping your fingers in a dish of vinegar, roll the meat mixture into walnut-size balls.

2. Melt the butter in a heavy 6-quart pot or Dutch oven. Add the meat-with-rice balls. Shake the pot so that the meat absorbs the butter aroma; do not brown the meatballs.

3. Add stock or water to cover. Bring to a boil and then simmer until rice is done. Taste. It is good to add liquid as needed, so that you have quite a bit left in the pot for the *avgolémono*; the rice absorbs the liquid, so make sure you check the level frequently. Keep the soup warm but not boiling.

4. Whip the egg yolks in a bowl. Add the lemon juice slowly, while whipping, and then a couple ladlefuls of pot liquid. Stir this sauce into the pot with the meatballs, gently, so that everything now looks creamy, thick, and lemony. Add ground pepper to taste. Serve hot.

5. This is truly comforting food on a cold rainy day. For children, I mash the balls with a fork. Serve with a salad and crusty bread.

- 1 pound extra-lean ground pork, beef, lamb, or a mixture
- 1 small onion, finely chopped
- 1/3 cup uncooked rice
- 1/4 cup snipped flat-leaf parsley
- 1 egg
- Salt and pepper
- 2 tablespoons butter
- 2 cups stock or water, or more as needed

For the finish:

- 2 egg yolks
- Juice of 1 lemon
- Ground pepper, to taste

Variation: For variety, I sometimes add yellow squash to this dish. Cut the slender neck off the squash, scoop out as much of the seed pulp as possible, and stuff the squash with the meat-rice filling. Then proceed as with the *yiouvarlákia* and the *avgolémono*.

Tart with Peppers and Mushrooms

Toúrta me Piperiés kai Manitária

For the crust:

2 cups flour

1 teaspoon yeast

2 tablespoons olive oil

2 teaspoons salt

1/2 cup plus 2 teaspoons warm water

For the filling:

6 scallions

4 peppers, yellow, red, green, and orange

8 ounces white mushrooms

10 cherry tomatoes

4 tablespoons olive oil

1 chicken bouillion cube diluted in 1/2 cup hot water

2 tablespoons snipped flat-leaf parsley

2 tablespoons snipped dill

Olive oil, for brushing

This recipe was given to me by my sister-in-law, Soula, and I share it here with minor alterations. It's colorful and aromatic and perfect as a side dish or for vegetarians.

Serves 8

1. Mix the crust ingredients thoroughly and shape into a ball. Cover and let it rest while you prepare filling.

2. Cut the scallions into rounds, the peppers into strips, the mushrooms into thirds, and the tomatoes in halves. Heat the olive oil in a very large frying pan or a heavy, wide casserole or Dutch oven. Sauté first the scallions, lightly, then add the peppers and sauté. You may need to do this in batches.

3. Add the mushrooms and the tomatoes to the peppers together with the dissolved bouillion. Stir well and cook until the peppers look wilted. Add parsley and dill. Make sure the vegetables are left with no water in the pot, just the sauce. Turn the heat off and allow them to cool.

4. Preheat the oven to 375°F.

5. Grease a round baking pan (I use my trusted 10-inch springform pan) and roll out the dough into a large circle to fit the bottom and come up the sides with an overhang of 1 inch. This is a very easy dough to roll out, especially if you use a slender dowel and turn it round and round. Transfer the dough to the pan and brush thoroughly with olive oil. Fill with the pepper mixture and fold the overhanging dough all around to make a rim. I roll it so that a fine scroll results. Brush all visible dough generously with olive oil. Bake in the preheated oven for 50 minutes. Cut in wedges and serve with slices of feta.

Rice with Dates

Rízi me Hourmádhes

4 scallions

4 tablespoons butter

1 cup basmati rice

1/4 cup blanched, slivered almonds

1/2 cup pitted dates, cut in thirds

1/2 teaspoon salt

This is delicious with pork or baked chicken (with thanks to my niece Lydia).

Serves 4–6

Sauté the scallions in the butter, then add the dry rice and stir to coat. Add 3 cups water, and the almonds, dates, and salt. Bring to a boil, cover, and let all the water be absorbed, about 30 minutes. Uncover, check the pot, and add 1/4 cup more water if rice is not quite done.

Variation: If you want a more exotic taste, add 1 teaspoon curry powder to the butter when sautéing, or a bit of cinnamon or nutmeg.

Yogurt Cake

Hálsema

In the charming university town of Chapel Hill, North Carolina, so beloved by the Tar Heels among whom I have lived for decades, there was a Greek restaurant named Mariakakis, after its owner. The ending *—akis* reveals a Cretan origin, and I have an affinity for the people of Crete. Mr. Mariakakis was a dear man who provided the Greek community of the Research Triangle with the cuisine of their homeland, and my daughter, a graduate student at the time, was very fond of him. Now he is gone, but his son transformed the place into a specialty foods market. The recipe most beloved by customers of the Mariakakis restaurant was a delicious yogurt cake. I have tried many yogurt cake variations, but this one is a winner. I am using it here to honor Mr. Mariakakis, with a few small alterations.

For the cake batter:

1 stick unsalted butter

Juice of 1/2 lemon

1/2 teaspoon baking soda

1 1/2 cups Cream of Wheat (not instant) or fine semolina flour

1 cup sugar

2 eggs

16 ounces Greek yogurt or sour cream

For the syrup and finish:

Juice of 1/2 lemon

Rind of 1/2 lemon, in strips

1 1/2 cups sugar

1 pint whipping cream

1 pint strawberries or raspberries

Serves 12

1. Preheat the oven to 375°F.

2. Melt the butter and let it cool a bit. Combine lemon juice and baking soda in a glass; keep in mind that it needs space because it will foam up. Combine the Cream of Wheat or semolina with the sugar.

3. In the mixer bowl place the eggs and beat them. Add the Cream of Wheat and sugar together with the melted butter. At low speed add the yogurt or sour cream and then the lemon-soda combination. Pour into a greased 13 x 9 x 2-inch baking pan. Bake in the preheated oven for 30 minutes.

4. Meanwhile prepare the syrup: Boil lemon juice and rind with sugar and 1 1/4 cups water for 15 minutes. Discard the rind. Cool the syrup.

5. When you take the cake from the oven, pour the cooled syrup on the hot cake and cover to steam until ready to serve. Whip cream, slice cake, and serve with the cream and fresh berries.

A Menu for Christmas Day

Winter Salad (*Himoniátike Saláta*) 170

Pork with Celery (*Hirinó me Sélino*) 172
or Stuffed Cabbage Leaves (*Lahanodolmádhes*) 171

Tart with Peppers and Mushrooms
(*Toúrta me Piperiés kai Manitária*) 174

Rice with Dates (*Rízi me Hourmádhes*) 176

Yogurt Cake (*Hálsema*) 177

❧ THE ROLE OF SWEETS FOR THE HOLIDAYS ❧

There is something to be said for rationing. It makes one so very grateful for special treats. During and after World War II, white sugar and other luxuries were rare and expensive. So baklava and the other marvelous traditional sweets identified with Greece were reserved for occasions like name days and holidays; in our family, they were the birthday party treats. That made one appreciate them all the more. Now they are found everywhere.

Since Greeks observe the religious seasons of the year quite faithfully, sweets are still made for holidays, not as simple desserts. (I am using the word "sweets"—*glyká tou tapsioú*, pastries baked in large, round pans—because this is the category in which the Greeks place all these baked goods that have a basic phyllo dough and a syrupy finish.) To this day, the final course of a meal in a Greek home is fresh fruit. These sweets called *glyká* are not considered desserts but are served with coffee as a separate and special eating occasion.

Christmas in Greece is celebrated more than in the past, but more commercially than religiously. New Year's Day, however, has always been a significant Greek holiday. Protochroniá, we call it, the first day of the year. Since it is a day for gift giving and also the day of Ayios Vasilis (St. Basil) who is a major saint in the Orthodox rite, everyone considers it a particularly important day. For every person named Vasilis, this is the celebratory name day—Vasilis comes from *vasiliás* (modern Greek pronunciation), which means "king" and is a very popular name in the country—so it's difficult to find a more significant holiday in the land.

Each person has his or her own recipe for these traditional sweets, and I have changed mine through the years. We may come from a collectivistic culture, but the recipes are always individualistic. And since these are the holidays, when a home should always smell of good things from the oven, I will give here a recipe that probably is more French than Greek, but it has an interesting history.

Copenhagen Pastry in Honor of a King

Copenhághê

For the bottom pastry crust:

1 stick plus 2 tablespoons butter

1 1/2 cups sugar

1 egg, slightly beaten

1 ounce brandy (optional)

1 1/2 cups all-purpose flour

1 1/2 teaspoons baking powder

For the almond filling:

8 eggs at room temperature

1/2 cup sugar

2 1/2 cups (12 ounces) blanched almonds, toasted and finely ground

1 teaspoon baking powder

1 1/2 teaspoons ground cinnamon

1 tablespoon brandy (optional)

A royal, elegant pastry that is found in the famous and ever-present sweet shops of Greece, Copenhagen is satisfying to make at home if you have the patience and ambition. Now, why would a Greek confection be called by a Danish name? This being Greece, it of course has a historical connection. After the long Ottoman occupation, the so-called Great Powers—England, France, and Russia—played chess with the obstreperous Balkans, most especially the emerging nation of Greece. Being the rulers of the European world and destiny, they imposed a Bavarian prince as king of the newly liberated, argumentative, and fractured Greeks. This German, King Otto, was deposed and succeeded by a Danish prince who became King George I of the Hellenes, after an election in which the Greeks, having a terrible time agreeing among themselves, or perhaps made insecure by centuries of occupation, voted in his favor. I grew up with such tales around our dinner table. My father's prodigious memory held dates and details and communicated them to us together with his passions. The young Danish prince, only seventeen when he became king of Greece, managed to reign for fifty years. No one else would have such longevity as ruler of Greece again, though political families would create dynasties that lasted just as long.

George, unlike his predecessor, was a modest man who enjoyed going about the city as a regular human being. He did well strolling the streets of Athens, but when in 1913 he visited my birthplace, Thessaloniki, a madman shot him in the back. A similar assassination in a street of another Balkan city would start World War I the following year. So goes the fate of the world.

George was beloved by many. Early in his reign a chef created this fancy pastry that bears the name of the king's birthplace, and a fine hotel in Athens, the King George, reminds us now of his story.

Makes 2 pans serving 10 each

1. Preheat the oven to 350°F.
2. Spray one 12 x 8-inch pan and one 10-inch round pan with cooking spray and set aside.

3. Make the pastry dough: In the large bowl of the stand mixer, cream the butter with the sugar until light colored. Add the egg and brandy; beat well. Mix flour with baking powder and add to the creamed butter. With your hand, mix it all together until you have a round ball of dough. Remove to a marble or work surface, knead just to make sure all flour is absorbed, and let it rest.

4. Make the filling: Clean the mixer bowl. In it beat the eggs with the sugar to a thick, creamy consistency. Add the ground almonds together with the baking powder, cinnamon, and brandy and stir until well mixed.

5. Flour a work surface or dust it with cornstarch. Roll slightly more than half the pastry dough into a rectangle to fit the first pan, and use the rest to fit your round pan. Pressing it with your fingers will help cover the bottom of the pan nicely. Pierce the crusts with a fork in several places.

6. Bake in the preheated oven for 10 minutes. Remove both pans from oven. Spread apricot marmalade or preserves on the pastry in the rectangular pan and berry preserves on the dough in the circular pan. Now spread the almond filling on top of both. Spread as evenly as you can, and don't worry if the preserves show on the edges.

7. For each pan, brush 5 sheets of phyllo dough lightly with melted butter (see page 14 on handling phyllo) and lay them on top of the filling, cutting the phyllo accordingly to fit the round pan. Score the phyllo into serving shapes. Bake at 350°F for 30 minutes.

8. Meanwhile make the syrup: Boil the sugar, water, and lemon for 10 minutes and then let the syrup cool to room temperature. When the baked pastries are cooled as well, cut partway down into diamond or square portions. Pour half of the syrup on each of the scored pastries, cover, and let them rest before cutting.

For the assembly:

8 ounces apricot marmalade or preserves

8 ounces berry preserves

10 sheets phyllo dough

2 tablespoons melted butter for brushing

For the syrup:

1 cup sugar

1 cup water

3 thin lemon slices

Christmas Cookies in Honey

Melomakárona

3 cups flour

1 teaspoon baking powder

1/2 cup organic shortening

1/4 cup butter

1/4 cup olive oil

1/2 cup sugar

1/2 cup orange and lemon
juice combined

Zest of 1 orange

1/4 cup brandy

1/2 teaspoon cinnamon

1/4 teaspoon ground cloves

For the syrup:

1 cup honey

1/2 cup freshly squeezed
orange juice

This is a greatly loved traditional Christmas cookie, but, like every-thing Greek, it has as many variations as the ancients had city-states. The word *melomakárona* needs no explanation to a Greek because *méli* is honey and the macaroon shape is long, even though there are many and complicated variations on this particular ety-mological root. However, why they are also called Phoeníkia I have not been able to discover, though I have tried. What I suspect is that the Phoenicians, who had many dealings with ancient Greeks, had something to do with it. There is a village in the Peloponnese by that name, however, so that may be a source. Names fascinate me, but this one defeats me. What remains agreed is that the result, regard-less of so many differences in ingredients, is delicious. This is a recipe handed down by people who came from Asia Minor, or from the Polis. I well remember the afternoon when I sat on my brother's veranda in Thessaloniki and the grandmother from the next apart-ment gave me her recipe for this cookie. Here is a light and rather easy version of that long-ago instruction.

Makes 30 cookies

1. Preheat the oven to 350°F.

2. Mix the flour with the baking powder.

3. Beat the shortening, butter, and oil at high speed in the mixer bowl together with the sugar. Beat until it looks quite light. With the mixer on low, add the citrus juices, orange zest, brandy, and spices and mix until well blended.

4. Now add the flour mixture a little at a time. After you add 2 cups, remove dough from the machine and work it on your favorite kneading surface. Be careful when adding flour; you don't want the dough to be heavy or hard, just workable. Shape into little sausages, press down to form ovals, then take a fork and press the tines almost to the bottom of the cookie to make designs. These indentations will stay through the baking. (Or you can leave the ovals as they are.) Bake in the preheated oven for 30 minutes, until the edges turn rosy.

5. While they are baking, bring the honey and orange juice to a boil
    and then turn heat off but keep it warm. When the cookies are out
    of the oven, place two at a time in a slotted spoon and dip into the
    syrup so that they are well coated. Remove to a platter.

6. When you have dipped all of them, pour the remaining syrup over
    them. Then roll each one in the syrup and place on another platter.
    In this manner you will have cookies that are sweet but not soggy.
    Most people sprinkle crushed walnuts on top, but I do not. You
    may want to mix some sugar with cinnamon to dust them with.
    Let them cool, and keep them in a tightly closed container; they
    last and improve in aroma and taste.

Shortbread Cookies
Kourabiédhes

1/2 pound best-quality unsalted butter, brought to room temperature

1 cup finely ground almonds (see step 1)

3/4 cup powdered sugar, plus about 2 cups for rolling

2 cups flour (approximate)

1/2 teaspoon baking soda or 2 tablespoons *alyssiva* (see headnote)

2 tablespoons brandy

Rosewater (see note below)

A Christmas table is never complete without *kourabiédhes*, our most beloved and characteristic offering. Thessaloniki is known for her superb *kourabiédhes* that come beautifully boxed. Don't fail to bring some back with you when you visit Greece. These cookies are thoroughly white because they are coated, repeatedly, in powdered sugar. There are two ingredients that are characteristic of Greek baking from ages past: baker's ammonia (ammonium bicarbonate), used in *koulourákia* (page 57), and *alyssiva*, used mostly in making *kourabiédhes*. Now both of them have been made redundant by the advance of baking powder and soda, but old-timers still use them. I have tried for years to find just the right consistency of ingredients so that my own *kourabiédhes* would taste like the ones I remember from Thessaloniki. The following recipe finally satisfied me enough to share.

Makes 3 dozen

1. Spread the almonds (I use peeled almonds) on a baking sheet and place under the broiler for about 5 minutes to turn a lovely rose color; don't let them burn. Cool and then grind them.

2. Preheat the oven to 325°F.

3. Put the butter in the mixer bowl with the 3/4 cup sugar, set it on high, and just let it rip while you prepare the rest. The butter will become very, very light and fluffy. While it grows in volume, measure the flour into a separate large bowl with the soda and keep it ready. Add the ground almonds to the butter mixture. Add the brandy and beat some more. Replace the wire whip of the mixer with the dough hook and gradually add 2 cups of the flour to the butter mixture; then remove the bowl from the machine and upend it on a work surface. The dough will be sticky, but be careful when adding more flour. Do it very gradually and keep feeling the dough to make sure it does not become dry. The amount of flour you add depends on the butter and how well you have whipped it. You want to just be able to handle the dough and shape it. Pinch a bit of dough, roll it between your fingers and then mold it into an oval or crescent shape. Do this with all of the dough. Place on parchment paper on a cookie sheet and bake in the preheated oven for 25 minutes.

4. While they are baking, sift lots of powdered sugar into a large pan with sides. Place a layer of hot cookies on this sugar and sprinkle with rosewater. Sift powdered sugar liberally over them. Repeat with the next layer. Let them cool. Then take each one and roll it in more sugar and place it in a tin with a cover. They keep a long time and improve in aroma and taste. This cookie has a special texture; it should crumble in your mouth. If it doesn't and it is chewy, try again!

Note 1: For those of you who are adventurous, here's what you do if you want to experiment with *alyssiva*, made from wood ash. Reserve about 1/4 cup from your fireplace ashes, put them in a cup of water, bring it to a boil, and then let it sit. When it has settled, strain the ash liquid by pouring it through cheesecloth placed on a tea strainer, or through a coffee filter, into a cup, and you have *alyssiva*.

Note 2: Rosewater is found in Middle Eastern stores or on websites. There is also an orange-blossom-flavored water, but it is too strong for my taste.

Chestnut Truffles

Kástana Troúfes

- 1 3/4 pounds boiled chestnuts (see note below)
- 3 tablespoons softened butter
- 1 1/2 tablespoons Grand Marnier
- 1/2 cup powdered sugar
- 1 tablespoon heavy cream
- 4 squares bittersweet chocolate, for dipping
- 1 cup shaved chocolate, for decoration

Recipes with chocolate are more French than Greek, though the Greeks have adapted many French words for their culinary purposes and recipes that suit them. Chestnuts, however, are grown and loved in Greece. I wanted to include something with chestnuts beyond the turkey stuffing, but they are all extremely rich and somewhat not in harmony with the tenor of this book. However, for those who love chocolate, here is an adaptation of a recipe that is not as rich.

Makes 30 truffle balls

1. Put chestnuts in a food processor, half of the amount at a time, and pulverize them with the butter, the Grand Marnier, the powdered sugar, and the cream. Refrigerate this pulp for an hour.

2. When you remove them, pinch a bit at a time and roll them into small balls.

3. To dip the truffles: Use a double boiler to melt the chocolate, keep it in a melted state, and, holding each ball with two forks, dip the chestnut balls into it. Then roll them in tiny chocolate pieces (this is what the Greeks call *troúfa*) and you have your chestnut truffles.

Note: For this recipe, I buy dehydrated chestnuts that come in 1-pound packages. After I boil them they weigh about 1 3/4 pounds.

Variation: A quicker and easier way to dip the truffles is to roll them in heavy cream and cover them in the chocolate pieces, omitting the melted chocolate dip. Place in little paper sleeves and serve.

Protochroniá: The Day That Begins the Year by Looking to the Past

Early darkness arrives with winter, and with the dark, fear. It is difficult for us, so bathed with the light of electricity, to imagine what it must have been like for ancient folk to experience the months of darkness covering their mountains and fields. Their homes were the only refuge of warmth and light, both emanating from the hearth. One of the most revered goddesses of polytheism was Hestia; the word *hestía* still means both hearth and home.

In Greek folklore, no time brings greater danger of harm and evil (which comes from open spaces like the chimney) than the Twelve Days of Christmas. Even modern Greece, secular and sophisticated, still retains vivid rituals aimed at counteracting the threat. These rituals started in forgotten, ancient times, slipped through the early centuries of Christianity, adorned themselves with some Christian essence, but have remained, at heart, thoroughly pagan.

Evil comes through the mean little creatures the Greeks called the *kalikántzaroi*, who dominate the dark and, jealous of family unity, invade the homes, trying to spoil foodstuffs and even clothing. In many Greek villages these spirits are called *paganá*, a strong etymological link to ancient paganism.

Within these twelve days of danger, the Greek Orthodox Church celebrates three religious holidays—Christmas on December 25, the circumcision of Christ on January 1, and Theopháneia (God's appearance) or Ta Phóta (the Lights) on January 6, the Epiphany of the Western church calendar. Yet little religious significance penetrates the persisting Greek rituals whose aim is to exorcise fears, to emphasize hope instead of despair, and to coerce Luck. Concerning this last: One of the less attractive rituals is the all-night vigil on New Year's Eve that is dedicated to gambling. In my childhood home, where no cards were ever played, I remember hearing the noises from the apartment next to ours as the neighbors gambled through the long night. Ours was a Protestant family; we considered gambling a sin, so for us it was a very strange ritual.

One of the most attractive and beloved rituals, universally practiced, is that of the Festal Bread. The baking and eating of festal breads takes place over the Twelve Days and beyond, but the best known is the New Year's bread, Vasilópita.

Protochroniá is the name for New Year's Day (*próton*, first, and *chrónos*, year), a holiday beloved of children for two reasons: the cutting of the Vasilópita and the exchange of gifts. Even though Christmas celebrations in the Mediterranean south have been affected by American images and northern European customs, the Greek villages and portions of city populations still retain the old meanings. Santa Claus, or Saint Nick, is totally foreign to Greek hagiography for this season (in Greece, St. Nicholas is associated with the sea). The saint who visits children on New Year's Eve is St. Basil, Ayios Vasilis in Greek, an actual early Church Father known for his generosity. St. Basil was from Caesarea in Asia Minor and is a strange choice for such a superstition-laden holiday: his writings and sermons were full of condemnation of astrology and omens, yet he has become the personification of good luck. He died in A.D. 379, on January 1. That coincidence made him the symbol of passage from the old year to the new, and therefore the symbol of new hope and promise.

Western Christmas carols were not known in Greece until recently. In fact, before television, which arrived late in Greece, it was the early Protestant choirs that brought the English carols to Greek ears. In Thessaloniki the choir started around the piano in our home, and later, instead of the carols called *kálanda* sung at this time, we would go from doorway to doorway singing Christmas carols in our Greek translation. The people loved them. We would arrive in the dark, in the entrance lobby of an apartment building, at the foot of the undulating terrazzo stairwell; our voices would rise in new, unfamiliar harmonies, with wonderful acoustics that enlarged the sound. Doors would open on floor after floor, and we would hear surprised murmurs and then applause. We would feel wonderful as we moved on.

New Year's *kálanda* are thoroughly Greek, sung by children during the day, their song usually accompanied by a simple iron triangle. In these, Ayios Vasilis is portrayed as a traveler on foot, carrying nothing but a walking stick. He comes from the depths of Asia Minor—recalling the thriving Greek civilization there in ages past— and he brings the alphabet, a confirmation that education for centuries belonged only to the clergy. When he is asked to sing, he replies that he knows no songs, only letters. The only magical thing about him is his walking stick; it sprouts branches on which the birds sing, representing fertility and abundance.

To this saint belongs the bread that bears his name, Vasilópita. The ancients too had a festal bread baked for the goddess Demetra, and breads sweetened with honey offered to their dead. Vasilópita seems to be a combination of the two. It is baked either in a very large round pan (*pita*) or in a braid (*kouloúra*). Inside the bread is hidden a coin for good luck.

On New Year's Eve at midnight the senior member of the household, with the family gathered round, cuts the *pita* in ritual fashion. First he makes the sign of the cross on it, then he cuts the portions clockwise in wedges, naming the first for the Virgin or St. Basil, followed by, in order, all the members of the family, present and absent, and then the home itself, the animals, and so on. It is thought that the person who gets the piece with the coin will have good luck in the coming year.

The lovely glazed surface of the Vasilopita and its orange-spice aroma recall to me all the magic of New Year's Eve—being allowed to stay up late, seeing all the lights go out to return at midnight, the deafening noise outside, and finally the loving wish "Chrónia Pollá," which means "May you be granted abundant years."

The very large round Vasilópita could not be baked at home. For years the Greeks took them to the public ovens where they were baked by an expert. These large breads (actually they are cakes) serve another function: They are an excuse for the yearly office party. The cutting of the Vasilópita is now practiced in every civic office and is the occasion for giving to charity. These parties start after New Year's and last well into January.

New Year's Bread
Vasilópita

7 cups unbleached flour

2 teaspoons baking powder

Zest of one orange, grated

1 teaspoon baking soda

2 cups freshly squeezed
orange juice

2 sticks plus 3 tablespoons
butter, at room temperature

2 1/2 cups sugar

8 eggs, separated

4 tablespoons brandy

You can make Vasilópita with yeast, but that tastes like *tsouréki* (page 5), or you can follow this traditional recipe that resembles a cake. In either case the round pan is a must because of the ritual of cutting wedges for every member of the family. If you cover a coin with foil and hide it in the dough, it will drop to the bottom and can be seen easily after cutting.

This bread will delight you with its aroma as much as its taste. It freezes well and is delicious lightly toasted.

Makes 15 wedges

1. Prepare a large round pan, 15 inches in diameter, by spraying it well with grease. Preheat oven to 375°F.

2. In a large bowl, mix the flour, baking powder, and orange zest.

3. In a good-sized pitcher, stir the soda into the juice; you need extra room because the soda will foam.

4. Cream the butter with the sugar and then add the egg yolks and beat well until very light and frothy. Add the brandy and then the orange juice.

5. In a separate bowl with a hand-held mixer beat the egg whites until they are firm, as for a meringue, but not dry. Add the egg whites and the flour mixture alternately to the liquids. The batter will be stiff but not hard.

6. Spread it in the pan and bake for 1 hour. Test for doneness by inserting a sharp knife in the thickest part. Cool in the pan and then remove to a cutting board; cover it with a white, preferably embroidered, cloth until time for cutting. Traditionally, the person doing the cutting scores the Vasilópita first, naming each piece for each family member present and all those who are absent. Serve with coffee or tea.

Bean Soup
Fasoládha

1 pound navy beans

2/3 cup good olive oil

1 1/2 cups chopped onion

1 carrot, chopped

2 stalks celery, leaves included, chopped

1 10.75-ounce can tomato puree

1/4 cup snipped flat-leaf parsley

Salt

Lemon juice, to taste

Freshly ground pepper

Years ago when I was young and thought I would never grow old, I used to play the piano and sing together with a group of older adults in a small North Carolina town. They had interesting stories to tell, stories that at times reminded me of Greek customs and superstitions. I helped them write their stories so that they could give them to their grandchildren. Most of the stories they told me dealt with New Year's Day's fears and their peculiar ways of exorcising the fears. One prevailing custom, then and now, is to eat black-eyed peas on New Year's Day. For the sake of those kind people who sang with me once upon a time, I will include here my favorite bean soup, one of the meals I missed the most when I left home. It was simple and homely and utterly comforting. When I finally returned home, I asked my dear stepmother to have it ready for me when I arrived. We don't use black-eyed peas but the smaller version of *ghíghantes*—those large white beans described on page 48. This was the traditional meal on washday in our home.

We used to consider dried beans poor people's food, but now that we know that legumes are good for our health, even fancy restaurants offer them in a variety of ways. I remember how surprised I was to find lentil soup on the menu of a very pricey restaurant in New York City. It tasted similar to mine, but the whole thing had been put through the blender and it was velvety smooth. *Fasoládha* is a soup for the winter months, and because it takes time to cook, the house fills with its rich aroma, a very homey, earthy bouquet.

Serves 10

1. Soak the beans for 12–15 hours in lots of cold water—they swell to three times their volume. Drain and rinse.

2. Use a deep pot. Add the oil, onion, carrots, and celery and sauté lightly. Add the beans and stir so that they are coated with the oil and mixed with the vegetables. (Do not add salt at this point.)

3. Add the tomato puree and water to cover the beans by at least 1 inch. Bring to a boil and then simmer for about 2 1/2 hours or until beans are tender. Now add snipped parsley and salt to taste.

4. Just before serving, add lemon juice. This is optional, but do try. The lemon brings out the flavor and has the additional benefit of allowing you to reduce the amount of salt needed. Freshly ground pepper is a must on this soup. A salad with good bread and cheese make for a complete meal.

Chicken Soup

Kotósoupa

1 whole stewing hen, free range

2 teaspoons salt

1 cup rice or orzo

1–2 bouillon cubes (optional)

2 yolks from free-range eggs

Juice of 1 lemon

Epiphany means winter, so I tend to think of soups and the comfort of something hot in the gloom of January. Many stories feature chicken soup as a cure for what ails . . . they have become a cliché, maybe because they have the imprint of experience. *Kotósoupa* features greatly in Greek traditional cooking, mostly because of the frothy finish, the *avgolémono*. When we were sick as children, we were given only broth with rice and lemon. We didn't like it because we were so used to the delicious *avgolémono*. Years later, my daughters would bring their school friends home just to taste this soup. Now these friends tell me that they are feeding their own children with my *soupa*; all of them asked for the recipe. My own grandchildren like it so much that when they were very little they demanded this "white soup" and nothing else. In fact, they learned to say *avgolémono* very early in their speaking accomplishments. Even today, whenever I make it, it disappears.

The etymology is: *avgó*, egg, plus *lemóni*, lemon. Once you master this sauce, you can use it in appropriate thickness in many different soups and in other dishes. Here is a basic recipe for *kotósoupa*. You may add other vegetables or pasta, but first learn the basics and then you can experiment.

Serves 8

1. In an 8-quart soup pot, place the hen and salt with cold water to

cover and bring to a simmer. Stew the hen slowly over low heat for a long time. When you cook it over very slow fire, the broth will be clear. Transfer it to a platter for another use.

2. Skim as much of the fat as you can, and then add rice or orzo. The tradition at home was to use rice for this soup. Children seem to prefer the orzo. Remember that either one will expand, so use 1 part rice or orzo to 4 parts liquid. You may want to add a bouillon cube or two, but this is personal preference. Keep adding liquid as needed.

3. Just before you serve the soup, prepare the *avgolémono*. First taste the broth and add more salt if needed. Keep the soup hot but not boiling. Whip the egg yolks thoroughly and then slowly add the lemon juice. Scoop a ladleful of the hot broth and pour slowly into the egg mixture, continuing to whip. Do this two or three times. (If something happens and the sauce curdles, just use one more egg yolk in the same manner to correct the mistake.) Then take this lemony froth and pour it into the soup. Stir and serve hot.

Chicken with Retsina Wine

Methysméno Kotópoulo

Retsina is a dry white wine with a resinated flavor. It is either loved or hated. Usually those who don't like it at first tasting will learn to like it if they persist and if they try it with savory Greek food. But in this recipe it simply adds a little something extra to the taste. (With thanks to my niece Phoebe.)

1 whole chicken, cut up

Juice of 1–2 lemons

Salt and pepper

Olive oil

1 cup retsina (if unavailable, use another dry white wine)

Serves 6–8

1. Place the chicken pieces in a bowl, pour half the lemon juice over them, salt and pepper them generously, and leave them for a few minutes.

2. Heat the olive oil in a pan. Picking up each piece of chicken with tongs, drain and reserve as much of the liquid as possible and place the chicken in the oil. Let all the chicken pieces brown nicely.

3. Pour the wine over them, and in 5 minutes pour the lemon juice from the bowl and the rest of the fresh juice into the pan. Lower the heat to simmer, cover, and let the chicken cook until done.

Chicken Roasted with Orzo

Kóta me Piláfi

1 whole stewing hen, free range

1/4 cup olive oil

Juice of 1 lemon

2 tablespoons dried tarragon or thyme

1 cup feta

1 cup orzo

Salt and pepper

Orzo is greatly loved by the Greeks. We make pilaf with it and use it to accompany both meat and poultry. Here is an easy and satisfying recipe from my stepmother.

1. Preheat the oven to 400°F.

2. Wash the hen well and reserve the insides for soup stock. Cut off all extra fat. Pat it dry.

3. Prepare an 18 x 12 x 2-inch baking pan by brushing the bottom generously with olive oil. Brush the hen with oil and lemon juice and place it in the center of the pan, breast side up. Sprinkle the cavity with the herbs and stuff it with the feta.

4. Pour the dry orzo all around the hen and carefully pour 3 cups water all around it. Season everything with salt and pepper. Pour the rest of the oil and lemon juice on the orzo and place the pan in the preheated oven. Roast until the orzo is soft and the chicken tests done, 2 hours. You may need to add more water to the orzo, so keep checking often. When you serve it, make sure everyone gets a portion of that delicious baked feta with the orzo.

Variation: Instead of orzo, surround the chicken with 6 medium potatoes cut in halves, 2 celery stalks cut in 2-inch lengths, and 6 small carrots. Omit the water, but do sprinkle lemon juice and olive oil over them.

Rice Pudding

Rizógalo

Serves 5

1. Boil the rice in a 6-quart pot with a pinch of salt in 1 1/2 cups water for 30 minutes; use more water if needed, but the rice should taste al dente. Place 1/4 cup of the cold milk in a cup, stir and dissolve the cornstarch in it, and set aside. Mix the sugar with the remaining milk and pour it over the boiled rice. Stir well.

2. Now add the dissolved cornstarch to the rice. Place over medium heat and cook, stirring often, until the liquids reach the boiling stage. Turn to simmer and keep stirring as the mixture thickens. Add the vanilla. The mixture doesn't have to reach the pudding consistency before you remove it from the fire. It will do so as it cools. Pour into serving glasses or bowls. Sprinkle with cinnamon or grated nutmeg. Serve warm, or refrigerate until ready to serve.

1/2 cup rice

Pinch of salt

2 cups milk, divided

1 tablespoon cornstarch

3 tablespoons sugar

1 teaspoon vanilla

Cinnamon or grated nutmeg

Potatoes with Sauce

Patátes Yiahní

6 potatoes

1/4 cup olive oil

1 onion, chopped fine

2 tablespoons grated celery root

2 garlic cloves, peeled and minced

2 large carrots, sliced thin

1 heaping tablespoon tomato paste

Salt and pepper

1 teaspoon oregano

We love potatoes served many different ways. One simple and delicious way to enjoy potatoes is to cook them in sauce, *yiahní* in the parlance. *Yiahni*, probably a Turkish derivative, refers to cooking in oil, onions, and tomatoes.

Serves 12

1. Peel the potatoes, cut them in serving pieces, and drop in a bowl with cold water to keep them from turning brown.

2. In the oil, lightly sauté the onion, celery root, garlic, and carrots. Add the tomato paste diluted in 1 cup water. Let all of the vegetables cook for 10 minutes. Now add the potatoes, one more cup of water, salt and pepper, and the oregano. Cover the pot and simmer for 1 hour or until the potatoes are easily pierced with a fork. The sauce should be thick and red, with all the water absorbed.

A Sample Menu for New Year's Day

Chicken Soup (*Kotósoupa*) 194

Chicken with Retsina Wine (*Methysméno Kotópoulo*) 195

Potatoes in Sauce (*Patátes Yiahní*) 200

New Year's Bread (*Vasilópita*) 190

Rice Pudding (*Rizógalo*) 199

Potato and Broccoli Soup (*Soupa Patátes me Bróccola*)

Fish Soup (*Psarósoupa*)

Lentil Soup (*Fakés*)

Stuffed Peppers and Tomatoes (*Ghemistá*)

Stuffed Leeks (*Prása Ghemistá*)

Sesame Breads from Thessaloníki
(*Kouloúria Thessaloníkis*)

Meatballs in Sauce (*Keftédhes me Sáltsa*)

Game Stew with Pearl Onions (*Stifádho*)

Puff Pastry (*Sfoliáta*)

Savory Pie (*Tyrópita*)

Chicken in Phyllo (*Kotópita*)

Meat Sausages with Ouzo (*Soutzoukákia me Oúzo*)

Homemade Halva (*Halvá Spitísio*)

Lemon Chicken with Potatoes
(*Lemonáto Kotópoulo me Patátes*)

Chapter 8

THE SEASON OF LIGHTS

*A*s you probably have noticed, the old saying "The Greeks had a word for it" rings true in cooking. But when it comes to holidays, this saying should be adjusted to "The Greeks have more than one word for it." This applies to the festival day the Western world calls Epiphany (which is also a Greek word); the Greeks call this time Ta Phóta (the Lights) and Theopháneia (God's appearance). Greeks are great believers in Luck; instead of making resolutions at the beginning of a new year, they tend to engage in activities that involve luck, and many spend New Year's Eve gambling with the hope that, if good luck finds them on that first day, it will last through the year.

❧ BAPTISM AND WATER SYMBOLS ❧

The church celebrates Theopháneia, God's appearance, over three days in its liturgical calendar. On January 5, worship centers on what the church calls the Great Hours (a litany) and the Great Sanctification: In the early years of Christianity, adults who had been instructed in the faith were baptized by the church on specific days—on the eves of Christmas, Epiphany, Easter, and Pentecost. The eve of Theopháneia/Epiphany, because of the commemoration of the baptism of Jesus, was most important. It's the day on which water is blessed to make the holy water used for baptism. Holy water is also used for sprinkling people and places in a ritual called *ayiasmós*, or sanctification. After the church service, when the family goes home to eat, the village priest and his acolyte who carries the holy water go from house to house; the priest dips the hyssop in holy water and sprinkles it on the door of each home and shop, every place where people live and work. The children run through the neighborhoods singing *kálanda* for this holy season: "Today appear the Light and the lighting, great joy and sanctity." And then the rhymes become utterly confused with folk myth and legend. This is also the time for the citizens to give offerings of money to the parish priest for the needs of the church.

The second day, January 6, is a holy day itself, Ta Phóta. The Western tradition focuses on the visit of the Magi to the Christ Child on this day; the Eastern Church focuses on the baptism of Jesus by John the Baptist, so the role of water becomes prominent on this day. The priests, bishops, and metropolitans, together with the populace, head for the waters of the village or the city. At the shore, the senior cleric throws a cross into the sea; young men, Boy Scouts and others, dive to retrieve it. One year I had the honor to be present as a journalist at the shore of Thessaloniki to see young Scouts in their rowboats, with their stunning choreography of oars, row out onto the waters of the Thermaic Gulf to accompany the divers. In the villages, people take the icons from their homes to wash them in the rivers. Overseas, if you live in a town anywhere that has a Greek community with its church, a town that happens to be near water, go out on January 6 to witness this unique custom.

The third day, January 7, is dedicated to the lonely prophet, John—the *Prodromos*, as the Greeks call him, "the one who goes ahead on the way," who lived in nature and baptized the people who came to hear him, calling them to repentance, "a voice crying in the wilderness." For some reason, the village tradition on this day focuses on the blessing of newlyweds by wetting them. This happens at the shore, where the couple is pushed into the waters and showered with wishes for the birth of children. (This is rather ironic in a country that now has a dangerously low birthrate.)

How fascinating it is to contemplate the origin of names for special days and the way some customs continue unchanged while others become encumbered or lost in new meanings.

Because Theopháneia falls in winter and this holiday is so associated with the gift of water, I naturally think of soups.

Potato and Broccoli Soup

Soupa Patátes me Bróccola

4 cups cubed potatoes (1-inch cubes)

1 pint stock

1 bunch broccoli (2 cups cleaned and chopped)

Pepper or lemon juice, to taste

Sometimes a recipe appears without planning, a happy accident that results in something delicious. It was January, cold and wet, and the freezer held containers of stock from the Christmas turkey. I took one out to thaw and looked around. What did I have in the refrigerator? Broccoli that needed to be cooked. My vegetable basket held quite a few potatoes. I like cream of broccoli soup but find it too rich. But this is an easy and delicious soup without the necessity for cream.

Serves 4

1. Boil the potatoes in the stock and 1 cup water.

2. In the meantime, clean, peel, and cut up the broccoli.

3. Let the potatoes get soft, filling with the flavors of the stock. Then add the chopped broccoli.

4. When the broccoli is soft, blend the mixture with a hand-held immersion blender. The blender does a good job without making the potatoes mushy.

5. Taste the broth, add a bit of pepper or lemon juice, and you're ready to serve.

Fish Soup

Psarósoupa

This may be my favorite winter meal, but it is difficult in a small town to find fish appropriate for a wonderful fish broth, so one has to improvise. As a child in Greece, I remember reading a poem in my first-grade reading book about a cat sitting on the windowsill smelling the aroma of *psarósoupa* and getting ready to yield to temptation. The rhymes still come to me from the distant past and make me smile as my memory smells the tempting aroma. I'll give you my favorite recipe. If you are lucky enough to find a fish with firm white flesh, so much the better. If not, mixing a variety of fish will do. After all, it was the ancient Greeks who first cooked what came to be called bouillabaisse; they called it *kakaviá*.

2 pounds whole fish, head(s) included

1 stalk celery with leaves, cut in two pieces

1 onion, peeled

1 carrot, scrubbed

A few sprigs of parsley

4 potatoes, peeled and cut into small pieces

1 teaspoon sea salt

1 teaspoon freshly ground pepper

3 egg yolks, at room temperature

Juice of 1/2 lemon

Serves 6–8

1. Wash the fish. If you are using several small fish, leave whole. Otherwise, cut the fish in large pieces and set aside.

2. Place the celery, onion, carrot, parsley, and sea salt in an 8-quart stockpot three-quarters filled with water. Simmer for 30 minutes.

3. Add the fish to the broth and cook until the meat is tender and opaque, about 30 minutes.

4. With a slotted spoon remove all solids from the broth and place on a platter. Discard the parsley and vegetables, but save the fish for later.

5. Place a clean 6-quart pot in the sink, put a colander or large sieve over it, and line it with a square of cheesecloth folded in four. If your colander has very small holes or if you are using a fine sieve, you can manage without the cheesecloth; or you can line the colander with a paper towel. Carefully strain the fish broth through this into the clean pot. You now have a clear, delicious, rich broth.

6. Place the pot with the broth on the stove and add the potatoes. Bring to a boil, then lower to simmer for 1 hour.

7. While the potatoes cook, carefully inspect the fish and remove any bones or skin. Cut what remains into bite-size pieces.

8. When the potatoes are soft, take your potato masher and mash them into the broth so that you have a thick soup.

9. Just before serving, add the cooked fish and stir gently. Heat until everything is steamy.

10. Finish with *avgolémono*: Whip the egg yolks and then slowly add the lemon juice while still whipping. Carefully scoop out a ladleful of the soup and whip it into the egg sauce. Repeat the process, then stir the egg mixture into the soup pot. Serve hot with freshly ground pepper.

Note: Mediterranean people do not discard the fish head; they declare that in it resides the flavor.

Lentil Soup
Fakés

1/2 cup olive oil

1 medium onion, chopped fine

2 carrots, sliced in thin rounds

1 celery stalk, cut up, leaves included

2 cups lentils, sorted and washed

3 ounces tomato paste diluted in 1 cup hot water

1/4 cup snipped flat-leaf parsley

2 teaspoons salt

1 teaspoon pepper

1/4 cup vinegar

I have a strong memory of my grandmother's lentil soup, which she would cook for us often when she lived with us after my mother's death. It had that distinctive vinegar smell and flavor and, like most soups, spoke of the simplicity and warmth of being at home. There are quite a few varieties of lentils available in the market today, and they all cook quickly and with minimal difficulty. No matter where they come from, I always pour the dried lentils onto a white plate and search through them to make sure that a little stone has not slipped through. Then I put them in a colander and wash them with cold water before starting the recipe.

Serves 8

1. In a deep pot, pour the oil and add the onion, carrots, and celery. Stir over high heat for a few minutes. Add the lentils and stir.

2. Now add 4 cups water and the diluted tomato paste. Let the lentils come to a boil, then lower the heat. In about 30 minutes, add the parsley, salt, and pepper. Keep adding water as needed while the soup simmers. Some water will be absorbed by the lentils and some will evaporate. If you like the soup with a lot of liquid, you should have at least two cups of liquid remaining when you finish. If you like it thick, don't add any more water.

3. When lentils are cooked—it doesn't take long, about an hour— pour the vinegar in the soup. Stir and serve.

❧ The Meaning of *Ladherá* ❧ in Greek Cooking

A myth beloved by my grandchildren is the battle between Poseidon and Athena for the heart of Athens. Which god would be chosen to be the protector of this remarkable city that would leave her imprint on the civilization of the whole Western world?

The people of Athens, so the myth goes, had chosen two finalists: the god of the sea and the goddess of wisdom. On the hill of the Acropolis, both the gods and the people gathered for the final vote. What do each of these gods have to offer us that is unique and that will benefit this city and her people? It was a crucial question, and the gods offered their best. Poseidon lifted his trident, strong and fierce, and struck the earth with it. Water gushed forth and formed into a well of seawater. (Another version of the myth says that Poseidon offered them the horse.) Then Athena struck the earth with her javelin and an olive tree sprouted. The people chose the olive tree and with it Athena, the goddess of wisdom, for she had offered them the better gift. This olive tree was reputed to have lived for a very long time, slipping from the memory of myth into historic retelling. (This is my favorite version of the myth, because it is the people and not the Olympians who do the choosing.)

The olive has nourished the Greek people for eons upon eons, and its origin, like the myth, is prehistoric. On the island of Crete, at the archaeological site of Knossos, the Minoan palace, there are rows of unearthed *píthoi*, wide-mouth earthenware pots, taller than a man, that were used four thousand years ago to store olive oil and other edibles. Ancient olive presses provide evidence of the way olives have been treated through the ages to yield their precious liquid, which Homer called golden.

Olive trees, ancient and gnarled, gray, twisted, hollow, and beloved, their silver leaves quivering in the breeze, cover much of the Greek earth. Victors were offered an olive branch; athletes cleansed themselves with oil; women used it for the beauty of their skin and hair. The wonderful oil so painstakingly produced has nourished us in thousands of ways. Doctors like Hippocrates and missionaries like St. Paul believed in its healing powers. The anointing with oil is known to readers of the Hebrew scriptures and is an integral part of the baptismal chrism in many Christian traditions, including the Greek Orthodox. At baptism, the priest, using olive oil, makes the sign of the cross on the forehead of the baptized.

Nothing equals good olive oil in the kitchen and at the table. The various families in my clan have their own source from particular village friends that are known for the excellence of their product. Buying olive oil should involve careful tasting by dipping a piece of bread in the oil sample, but that is probably not possible in most places. Greeks consume more olive oil per capita than any other nation. They also produce the greatest percentage of extra-virgin: 80 percent of the oil produced in Greece is extra-virgin. The taste and color depend on the geographical location. The question as to which is the best olive oil—Greek, Italian, or Spanish—verges on political arguments, so you have to make your own selection. Make sure the oil has very low acidity; below 1 percent is best.

Oil that is produced on the island of Lesbos, also known as Mytilene, is remarkable for its yellow-gold color and rich aroma. The island of Crete (Kriti to the Greeks) produces superb oil—look for the one from Sitia. The same is true for Kalamata, already well known for her olives; and, of course, a bit north of there in the Corinthian plain there is lovely oil. There are more locations, but I don't have space for them, they are so numerous. The Greeks are really passionate about the origin of the olive oil they consume.

The modern Greek word for oil is *ládhi*. In my city in the north, in Thessaloniki, a famous neighborhood carries this name Ladhádhika. Near the port, it was one of the few neighborhoods that didn't burn in the terrible fire of 1917. At that time it was filled with Jewish businesses, but after the fire it went into decline and became a place of ill repute. In the 1970s the buildings were restored and it became a place for the young, filled with bars, restaurants, and music. But the name remains to remind us of the storing of this precious liquid.

The word *ládhi* is the root for a whole way of cooking, *ladherá*, which means cooked with oil. In a country of very hot summers, it was necessary to cook foods that would taste good when cooled. So all vegetables and legumes were cooked in oil, which, unlike butter, does not change its taste and texture when cooled. For summer meals we had green beans, okra, peas, eggplant, artichokes, and other greens and salads cooked or dressed in sauces that had olive oil as their base. Many of these dishes utilized a favorite way of preparing a whole meal in one pan—stuffed vegetables. We find many interesting and imaginative ways to stuff squash, eggplant, tomatoes, and peppers. We even stuff cabbage and grape leaves.

So the history and reality of olive oil are as much a part of Greek culture as the presence of the sea and the mountains. For both ancient and modern Greeks, the olive tree is sacred.

Stuffed Peppers and Tomatoes

Ghemistá

I have a strong connection to this dish, because it was the first meal I ever cooked—well before I learned anything about creating a recipe. And after finishing that particular, out-of-time assignment, I did not cook again for many years to come.

I mentioned in the introduction that as a schoolgirl I was not expected to do much in the kitchen beyond the occasional washing of dishes. So preparing these stuffed vegetables was an exception in my young life—an adventure, and a result of terrible loss.

I was only eleven when my mother died, and the burden of cooking for five people fell on my older sister, who had just turned sixteen. On this particular occasion she had gone to Athens to stay with a friend, something we all applauded because she needed a vacation from us and from the responsibilities thrust upon her young shoulders.

Before leaving for work, my father gave me detailed instructions. I listened very carefully because, even though I was a fast learner, I had never been in charge of the kitchen before and I was nervous and apprehensive. The greengrocer arrived early from his village; he walked down our street in the morning, the fresh vegetables spread out in open boxes on a flat cart pulled by a tired mule. He sang out the names of his vegetables in a melodic big voice. My task that morning was to find large, firm tomatoes, well-shaped green peppers fit for stuffing, a couple of onions, and one bunch of parsley. Dad had left the appropriate number of drachmas for that purchase. Then, in a kitchen tiled in red, I, trembling, would prepare the day's meal. I remember the apprehension that accompanied me, the arrangement of the colorful vegetables in the *tapsi*, a deep round pan lined with shiny copper on the bottom (my mother had been so proud of her shining pan). I don't remember taking the filled *tapsi* to the public oven, and none of the family's comments stayed with me. But I do know that the next time I cooked this particular dish, I was a grown woman and a mother.

The smell of the vegetables as they baked in the oven in my own home, that sharp, familiar aroma of pepper roasting in olive oil, brought back that very young effort, the terrible feeling of loss that accompanied everything we did during those days, the feeling of inadequacy. I kept my tears to myself, and when I told the story to my children I tried to make a joke of it—my childish fear of cooking. Here, then, is a basic recipe that leaves you lots of room for experimentation.

5 bell peppers

5 large tomatoes

1/2 cup good olive oil, or more to taste

Salt

1 large onion, finely diced

2 cups uncooked long-grain rice, *not* the fast-cooking kind

4 mint leaves or basil, snipped

1/2 cup snipped flat-leaf parsley

Pepper, to taste

Serves 5 as main dish, 10 as side

1. Preheat the oven to 400°F.

2. Choose a baking pan about 2 1/2 inches deep and large enough to hold the peppers and tomatoes in snug rows. The vegetables do well when they are side by side holding each other up. Pour enough good olive oil to cover the bottom. Set it next to you as you proceed.

3. Cut a slice off the top of each vegetable so that you create a cap for each pepper and tomato cup. Set the caps aside. Remove the seeds of the peppers, rinse, and place in the pan, open side up. Carefully scoop out the interior of each tomato and reserve the pulp. Place the tomato cups among the peppers in the pan. Sprinkle them all with salt and then pour a tablespoon of olive oil in each one. Set aside while you prepare the filling.

4. In a deep 12-inch frying pan or a wide pot, sauté the onion in 1/4 cup olive oil until golden. Add the dry rice and stir well. Chop and add the reserved tomato pulp, along with mint or basil and parsley. Sprinkle with salt and pepper. Stir. Now add enough water to cook the rice, 5 cups to begin with. Bring to a boil, lower heat, cover, and simmer until water is absorbed. Taste for doneness; it should be just al dente. Add more water and cook longer if necessary. Taste and add more salt and pepper if needed—rice requires quite a bit of salt.

5. Carefully, with a scoop or deep spoon, fill each tomato and pepper with the rice mixture, leaving a 1/2-inch space on top for expansion. Pour a teaspoon of olive oil and a tablespoon of water into each rice-filled veggie. (When I have more filling than vegetables to fill, I spoon it between the veggies. It is delicious and the children prefer it.) Cover the vegetables with their individual caps. Pour 1/2 cup water into the pan.

6. You may prepare all this ahead and refrigerate until 1 hour before serving.

7. Bake in the preheated oven for 45 minutes. Remove from oven 15 minutes before serving. This is a good vegetarian dish when accompanied by bread and cheese. Feta blends wonderfully with these flavors. In the summer, the Greeks eat this meal not hot but at room temperature.

Variation: For something more exotic, many cooks add pine nuts and raisins.

Stuffed Leeks

Prása Ghemistá

The versatile leek, long regarded a food for the poor, can provide elegance in recipes with its texture like silk and its creamy quality when mixed with other ingredients. Greece produces both the very slender leeks that can be eaten whole and the thick, large variety with rich, long white stalks.

3 large leeks

1/2 onion, chopped

1/2 cup olive oil, halved

3/4 cup rice

Salt and pepper, to taste

1/2 cup snipped parsley and dill combined, or fennel fronds

1 whole lemon

Serves 6 as a side dish

1. Cut off the leeks' dark green tops and even the medium green; then cut off the remaining root at the very tip. The leek, being an onion, is made up of multiple layers wrapped tightly around each other. Slit the white parts vertically, but just to the heart, then hold them under the faucet to wash each layer free of sand. Spread the cut open to remove the inner core. This heart of the leek is quite firm; reserve to use for the sauce. One leek yields about five usable cylindrical layers for stuffing (they close by themselves to form a cylinder even after cutting). Now cut the leeks in two horizontally, doubling the number of casings.

2. Chop the hearts of the leeks and sauté them with the onion in 1/4 cup oil. Add the rice and stir to coat thoroughly, then add 2 cups water. Simmer until the water is almost absorbed. Add salt and pepper and herbs. Stir and simmer a few more minutes until all the water is absorbed.

3. Fill the leeks with the mixture, leaving room for expansion of the rice.

4. Coat the bottom of a heavy 10- to 12-inch frying pan with oil. Place the filled leeks in it side by side. Pour the remainder of the oil and 1/4 cup water carefully into the edges of the pan. Cover with an upside-down plate to keep the leeks more or less closed, then cover the pan and simmer until done, about 40 minutes. Make sure the heat remains low, because leeks are delicate.

5. When they are cooked, remove them very gently to a serving platter. Don't worry if some of the filling has escaped. Add it to the platter, then squeeze the juice of a lemon into the cooking pan, scrape all the good-tasting remnants, and pour over the dish.

Variation: As with other stuffed vegetables, you may vary the filling by adding ground meat, but I prefer just the rice.

Sesame Breads from Thessaloníki

Kouloúria Thessaloníkis

2 teaspoons yeast

1/4 cup plus 1 tablespoon sugar

2 pounds plus 1/4 cup flour

5 tablespoons corn or olive oil, or a mixture

2 cups sesame seeds

Thessaloniki is loved by her inhabitants. When they speak of her, the citizens sound like people in love, and the songs they sing of her are indeed love songs. Though the city is now very large and greatly spread out into many neighborhoods, there is still the feel of a small village. Her name is that of a woman—the half sister of Alexander—so the city is thought of only in feminine terms. For those of us who have seen her changed so drastically, childhood memories keep us from losing heart at the noise and the traffic. How easily we used to walk her streets and in such blissful safety, even at night.

As an imaginative child I used to watch the people who walked under my balcony every day. Early in the morning a man carrying his small bakery in his arms would appear around the corner, singing out, "Kouloúria! Zestáa kouloúria!" On the balcony we kept a basket at the end of a rope; we would lower it with drachmas in it and he would place the *kouloúria* inside, slender breads covered in sesame. They are called *kouloúria* because they are round. Together with hot tea they served as breakfast or snack. They still do.

We never made our own, because they were so readily available in the market, but here is a recipe that comes close to the remembered smell and taste.

Makes 20 *kouloúria*

1. In a large bowl dissolve the yeast, 1 tablespoon sugar, and 1/4 cup flour in 1/2 cup warm water no hotter than 110°F. Cover with a tea towel and let it rest until it bubbles. Then add, alternately, the rest of the flour and sugar, the oil, and about 2 1/2 cups warm water to form the dough. Knead until smooth. Cover and let it double in size—an hour or so.

2. Preheat the oven to 400°F.

3. Set out two wide, shallow bowls, one containing water and the other the sesame seeds.

4. Take the dough, a pinch at a time, and roll it into ropes about 12 inches long and no thicker than your finger. Take these dough ropes, one at a time, and dip them into the water quickly, shake the drops off, and then roll into the sesame until thoroughly covered.

5. Bring the two ends together to form a circle. Place on parchment paper, about six on a cookie sheet. Bake in the preheated oven for 10–15 minutes. Try them with coffee. They are delicious hot or cold. They freeze and reheat well.

❦ The Last Season ❧
Approaching Lent with Family Favorites

The month of January is closely associated with the liturgical season of Ta Phóta, Epiphany, when office groups, reunion classes, and clubs continue "cutting the *pita*," a ritual that starts on New Year's Day and continues all month. As February begins, the miracle of flowering almond trees reminds Greeks that spring is near. With the ending of winter they think of Apokries, the Greek carnival, something like Mardi Gras. More celebrated in certain cities, it is a time for fancy costumes, parades, and confetti.

The cities of Patras in the Peloponnese and the city of Rethymnon in Crete are famous for their Apokries, a strong remnant of past Venetian presence. My clan, being Protestant, avoided these "worldly" festivities, but I remember begging passionately for a traditional Greek costume to wear to the school party, a wish my mother granted before her death. I still have the picture of a rather sad child dressed like a village Greek of the nineteenth century looking wistfully at the camera. That was the extent of my Carnival participation—that and throwing confetti.

I have been a professional woman most of my life, but nurturing and feeding my family has always been my primary focus. I delighted in feeding my daughters and husband, but nothing has been more fun for me than preparing meals for my grand-children. The little boys who live away from me and spend two weeks in the summer with us are asked by friends back home, "What do you do at your Mika's house?" Their answer: "We eat." Fortunately, they are both slender and energetic, so I enjoy cooking what they like without worries about their weight. This segment is dedicated to my family's favorite meals. They are created with love and care, not for show-ing off but for nourishment and comfort. Eating together remains one of the joys of family life. Together with music, good food has kept us in joy together.

It is my wish that, when you try these recipes, you will have the blessing of eating with your family, of remembering and telling stories, and thus creating your own rituals.

Meatballs in Sauce

Keftédhes me Sáltsa

My daughter Niki doesn't eat red meat now, but this was her favorite meal as a child.

Serves 6

1. Mix all the meatball ingredients. Blend together but do not knead. Let the mixture rest for a while.

2. Set out a bowl of flour for dusting the meatballs. Have a small bowl of vinegar nearby.

3. Pinch a bit of the mixture, roll into a walnut-size ball, and place on a holding platter. Dipping your fingers in the vinegar to keep them from sticking, continue until all the meat is used. Flour the meatballs by placing them, a few at a time, in the bowl and rolling them around until well dusted.

4. In a frying pan, heat enough oil to cover the bottom third of the meatballs. Brown the meatballs in two batches so that there is room for turning them. By the time they are browned all around, the insides are cooked also. Remove each batch to absorbent paper towels.

5. Prepare the sauce: In the olive oil, sauté the diced onion. Add the tomatoes and 1 cup water; stir well. Let the mixture come to a boil. Reduce heat. Add the sugar, oregano, salt, and pepper, and let it all simmer for at least half an hour.

6. Place the *keftédhes* in the sauce; heat well. This may be served with any pasta or rice, but our family's favorite was to eat it with potatoes that had been quickly crisped in oil and then added to the sauce to soften. Children love this dish.

Note: In the summer, it is much better to use ripe, fresh tomatoes peeled and put through the food mill. You may increase the tomatoes and add some water, but do not add tomato sauce or paste.

For the meatballs:

1 pound ground meat of your choice

1 finely chopped onion

1/2 cup soaked bread (day-old baguette, not white sandwich bread)

1 teaspoon salt

1 teaspoon pepper

3 cloves garlic, mashed

1 1/2 teaspoons ground cumin

1 teaspoon oregano

1/4 cup finely snipped parsley

1 tablespoon olive oil

Flour for dusting

Vinegar for dipping fingers

Oil for frying

For the sauce:

1/4 cup olive oil

1 onion, chopped

1 14.5-ounce can tomatoes, or 2 large ripe ones (see note)

Pinch of sugar

1 tablespoon oregano

Salt and pepper

Game Stew with Pearl Onions
Stifádho

For the marinade (for game only):

Equal amounts water and vinegar, to cover the meat

1 large carrot, sliced

1 celery stalk, cut up

1 onion, cut up

1 leek, cut up

2 tablespoons parsley

3 pounds hare or rabbit or other meat (see note)

2 pounds pearl onions

1/2 cup olive oil

1/2 cup Mavrodaphne wine or port

2 tablespoons vinegar

3 heaping tablespoons tomato paste diluted in 1 cup water, or 3 ripe tomatoes, peeled and mashed

2 bay leaves, cut in two

3 allspice berries, or 1 clove

2 cloves garlic, or more to taste, peeled

1 teaspoon sugar

Salt and pepper, to taste

When I taught creative writing to high school students, I used to try to communicate to them the power of the evocative use of memories. They did not understand the words. So I would ask about their favorite food: "Describe to me the smell, the atmosphere of a smoke-filled pig pickin' or the taste of fried chicken dinners at your grandmother's," I would suggest.

That was too simple, they said. Creative writing should be about romantic places they had never seen, about adventures they could only imagine. But imagination was so tainted by television that it did not move even their own emotions.

"Yet," I would insist, "if you make me long for what you experience at your grandmother's, here in this little town, you will have succeeded as a writer. Someday you will smell a flower, and it will remind you of a visit to the country, or you will taste something ordinary, but it will remind you of a day at a relative's home, and then all that you felt on that day will come rushing back to you."

Ah . . . recognition would visit their eyes, and they would bend over the paper.

Just that much of a suggestion, I thought, was enough at that stage. I did not want to reveal to them that as we grow older and further removed from our childhood, smell and taste have the audacity to attack us with the sudden pang, the déjà vu, the almost mystical power of transporting us to the past, and with pain.

So it is with me and the aroma of *stifádho*. Is it, I wonder sometimes, that my childhood was so dramatic because of the world events propelling all of us at that time to the shaking of our foundations, that the war and misery of it make me more susceptible to such smells and memories?

Perhaps not. I think it has more to do with simple things, like the memory of my mother at the kitchen sink—one of the rare memories of her healthy years— the sniff of something that brings that other world back, a world where windows remained open to the outside, where the atmosphere was not purified by air conditioners and the heat came from burning wood and not from unseen vents, where food was cooked for most of the morning for a leisurely afternoon meal and uninhibited conversation.

There are many aromas and tastes that bring back the sudden memory, the almost unbearable feeling of being a child in a country where life was much simpler and the future was still an unknown. But some are so distinctive that just to think about the word brings back the memory.

That word is *stifádho*, and I probably did not like the heavy aroma and the onion when I was a child. Now I would consider it a choice meal for a winter day, when the house becomes redolent of good and pleasant things.

Stifádho in old Thessaloniki always meant *lagós stifádho*, hare stew, but it can be made from any game or domestic meat. A few ingredients are standard—the pearl onions, the *daphne* (bay leaf), the marinade, the heavy sweet wine—but there are no hard and fast rules, and you can experiment to your own taste. Do plan ahead, though. If you are using game, it needs a day to marinate. And remember that *stifádho* is much better when cooked a day before serving.

Serves 8

1. If using hare or other game, combine the marinade ingredients and marinate the meat for 24 hours in the refrigerator. On cooking day remove the meat, wash in cold water, and pat dry.

2. Peel the pearl onions. If you drop them in boiling water first, they peel easily. Leave them whole.

3. Heat the oil in a deep frying pan or heavy casserole. Quickly brown the pieces of meat, a few at a time, and remove to a plate. At this point, many cooks also brown the onions. This is optional; I do not.

4. In the already hot pan or casserole, pour the wine and vinegar and the diluted tomato paste. Stir, scraping the bottom. Return the meat to the pan. Simmer for at least 30 minutes. Place the pearl onions on top, adding the bay leaves, allspice, garlic, sugar, and salt and pepper. Cover the pan and cook on medium heat for another 30 minutes, shaking the covered pan.

5. Turn the heat to low and simmer until the meat can be cut easily with a fork, about 1 hour more. The sauce should be thick, not runny. Uncovering the pan at the end allows it to reduce. Check frequently, so that it does not dry out and the meat does not stick to the pan. Add more wine or water if needed. Shake the pan carefully. Remove the bay leaves and allspice before serving. Serve with plain rice. The sauce is delicious with it.

Note: In place of game, you may substitute veal, pork, and lamb combined. Or other types of game may be used—venison, pheasant, guinea fowl. On a hare or rabbit, the usable meat consists chiefly of the two thighs and the saddle.

Puff Pastry

Sfoliáta

10 ounces good butter, divided into fourths

4 cups flour

2 teaspoons baking powder

1 tablespoon salt

1/2 cup oil

1 egg, beaten, for the egg wash (see next page)

Members of my family have all agreed for years that my sister-in-law Soula makes the best *pites* and that it has to do with her pastry. So finally I asked her for her recipe, and she graciously shared it with me. It takes just a little time, but it is quite simple, and it rolls out beautifully. The results are so satisfying that you may not want a different crust for a while. The Greeks call this pastry *sfoliáta*, from the Italian *sfoglia*. The amounts are for a very large *pita*, the kind that is baked in the enormous round Greek pans. But since the dough is formed in two squares, you can use one for the top and bottom crusts of a more modestly sized rectangular pie, freezing the other square for later use.

Homemade puff pastry is delicious with all the Greek *pita* fillings found in this book.

Makes crusts for one 15-inch round *pita* or two 14 x 9-inch *pites*

1. Put the butter in the freezer while you assemble the rest. The butter needs to be very cold and hard.

2. Mix the flour with the baking powder and salt. Add the oil and 1 cup water. You may need additional water, as much as 1/4 cup, but add only enough to make the dough pliable. After kneading for 10 minutes, cut the dough in two balls, wrap them, and refrigerate for about an hour (or up to 24 hours).

3. When ready, take one-fourth of the butter out of the freezer and cut it into small pieces. On a well-floured surface, roll out one ball of dough to make a square of about 12 inches. Dot the dough with one-fourth of the cold butter. You don't have to spread it; it's too hard: just press it in with your palm. Fold the dough in half, then in half the other way, so that you have a square one-fourth of the original size. Roll this out to the original dimensions. This will press the butter into the dough. Now repeat the process of dotting the dough with a fourth of the butter and folding it in half first one way and then the other. Set this folded dough aside.

4. Perform the same procedures with the other ball of dough and the rest of the butter. You are now in possession of two potential sheets of pastry.

5. Cover and refrigerate while you assemble the filling.

Savory Pie
Tyrópita

Makes 1 tyrópita

1. Preheat the oven to 400°F.

2. Butter or spray a 14 x 9-inch baking pan. Divide the dough, roll out the bottom crust, and place it in the pan.

3. Mix the cheeses together, then fold in the yogurt. Add 4 eggs and stir to mix well. Add the dill and mix again. Spread the filling on the bottom crust in the pan.

4. Roll out the second crust and lay it over the filling. Fold the edges well and brush everything with the remaining beaten egg. Score the top lightly into serving portions. Bake for about 50 minutes or until the top is rosy. Serve hot.

1 square of *sfoliáta* dough (page 222)

1 pound feta, crumbled

1/2 cup grated Parmesan

1/2 cup thick Greek yogurt

4 eggs, slightly beaten, plus 1 for brushing

1/4 cup fresh snipped dill

Note: Within this pastry crust you may use any of the fillings, both savory and sweet, found in this book.

Chicken in Phyllo

Kotópita

2 scallions, sliced thin

2 stalks of celery, cut into very small pieces

1 stick of butter, plus 2 tablespoons for sautéing

3 cups chopped cooked chicken

1/4 cup chicken broth

1/2 cup snipped parsley and dill combined

Salt and pepper

1 egg, beaten

1/2 pound phyllo dough, at room temperature

1 cup crumbled feta

My granddaughter, Alexandra, loves Greek culture and Middle Eastern cuisine and is fast learning to enjoy cooking. Of all her favorites, she picks *kotópita*.

Note: Before working with phyllo, please see advice on its handling, page 14.

Makes 15 portions

1. Preheat the oven to 350°F.

2. Sauté the scallions and celery lightly in 2 tablespoons butter. Add the chicken and broth and stir until the liquids are absorbed. Add the herbs and salt and pepper. Set aside. When cool, add the beaten egg to hold it all together.

3. Melt the stick of butter over low heat.

4. Open the package of dough and, working quickly, brush each sheet with butter before placing it in a 14 x 11 x 2-inch metal baking pan. Use 10 sheets of dough for the bottom crust. Spread the cooled filling on it, then crumbled feta. Cover with the rest of the phyllo, buttering each sheet lightly and quickly. Brush the top one thoroughly with the melted butter.

5. Now score the *pita* into diamond shapes or rectangles and bake in the preheated oven for 45 minutes.

Variation: After years of using phyllo for this *pita*, I made puff pastry (see page 222) and enclosed the filling in it. The dough for the bottom crust came up the sides of the pan and half covered the filling. Then I rolled out the remaining dough in a smaller circle than the pie pan for the top crust and brushed it with egg yolk. It turned a lovely color, beautiful to look at and very satisfying.

Meat Sausages with Ouzo

Soutzoukákia me Oúzo

My grandson Luke is tall and slender. He used to eat very sparingly, so when he was little I created this recipe for him. When children refuse to eat, dip a piece of bread into this sauce and offer it to them; they will quickly ask for more. *Soutzoukákia* means little sausages, but this refers only to the shape of these oblong meatballs.

Serves 8

1. Combine the meat, cumin, salt, and pepper, and mix lightly. Pinch off bits of the mixture and form them into sausage shapes about 2 inches long and 1 inch in diameter. (I pinch the edges so they are thicker in the middle.)

2. Melt the butter in a frying pan, add the *soutzoukákia*, and brown lightly. Away from the fire, pour the ouzo into a small cup. Add this liquid to the pan. (Be careful: Ouzo has a high percentage of alcohol and can flare up if drops fall onto the open flame.) Shake the pan; the alcohol will evaporate and only the flavor will remain.

3. Add the tomato sauce, sugar, and 1 cup water. Stir well. Add the oregano, reduce the heat to simmer, cover, and let the *soutzoukákia* absorb the flavors.

4. When they are cooked, they should be in a very thick red sauce. During the cooking, add more water if it is needed, but it will all evaporate. Serve with pasta, rice, or potatoes.

1 pound extra lean ground sirloin or chuck

1 teaspoon cumin

1 teaspoon salt

1 teaspoon pepper

2 tablespoons butter

1/4 cup ouzo

1 14.5-ounce can tomato sauce

1 teaspoon sugar

1 tablespoon oregano

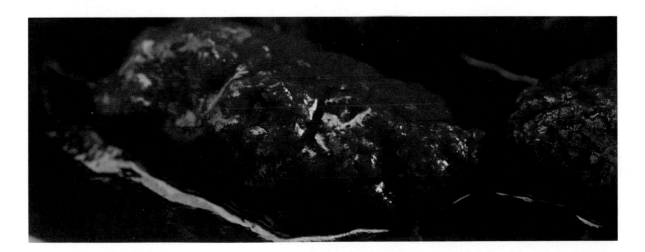

Homemade Halva

Halvá Spitísio

From early on, my grandson Jeremy was willing to try different recipes and tastes. He told me that it is difficult for him to pick a favorite, but even when he was tiny he could pronounce "halva" and ask for it. So this is for Jeremy.

Halva falls most definitely in the category of comfort food. It was one of the first pudding-like desserts all my grandchildren liked when very little, and one of them called it "my cinnamon." That was the ultimate description of it for me—that the children accepted it as their own, that I made it just for them, and that cinnamon was the one ingredient they could remember, a spice for the ages.

Don't confuse this with store-bought halva, which has a different consistency and is mostly made of sugar.

For the syrup:

4 cups water or 2 cups water with 2 cups milk

2 cups sugar

1 stick cinnamon

3 cloves

1 finger-length lemon peel

1 1/2 sticks unsalted butter

2 cups Cream of Wheat (not the instant kind) or coarse semolina flour

1/2 cup ground almonds

2 tablespoons sesame seeds

Cinnamon for dusting

Serves 10–12

1. Prepare a 10-inch fluted cake pan by spraying it with cooking spray. Set aside. In a 4-quart pot bring to a boil all the syrup ingredients, stirring until sugar melts, and then keep just at a simmer.

2. In another large, heavy pot with a handle (I use a copper 6-quart pot), melt the butter over low heat, add the Cream of Wheat or semolina, almonds, and sesame, and start stirring. This step makes all the difference. You want the dry ingredients to turn brown slowly, slowly. The wonderful aroma of sesame and almonds toasting together with the wheat will fill the kitchen. Be patient so that nothing burns but everything is toasted. (I use both a wooden spoon and an egg whisk alternately to make sure everything turns over well and is touched by the butter.)

3. From the syrup pot, with a slotted spoon, remove the aromatics. Keeping the heat under the Cream of Wheat at low, pick up the syrup pot by the handle and—carefully!—pour the syrup into the dry ingredients. Protect your arms and face from splatters. Whip the syrup into the solids with the egg whisk so that there are no lumps left. The dry ingredients will absorb all the liquid while you stir, and the whole thing will bubble mightily and move away from the sides of the pan. When that happens, pour or scoop the halva into the fluted cake pan. When you are ready to serve, turn it over onto a platter and sprinkle with cinnamon. It is delicious when warm—children love it—but it can be eaten cold also.

Lemon Chicken with Potatoes

Lemonáto Kotópoulo me Patátes

2 chicken breasts, cut into bite-size pieces

4 tablespoons butter

Juice of 1 lemon

4 potatoes, peeled and sliced into very thin rounds (see note)

Salt and pepper

My littlest grandchild, Miles, like the rest of the children, is thoroughly international in his tastes and possesses an enviable palate. When he was only four he was praising *dolmadhákia* and mussels, and by age five he was eating sushi. But for his favorite he chose true comfort food, something I created for him because he is so fond of potatoes and he can afford to store more calories.

Serves 6

1. Brown the chicken in 2 tablespoons of the butter and then douse with half of the lemon juice. Remove to a platter.

2. Add the remaining 2 tablespoons of butter to the pan, then the potatoes. Flip the slices with a spatula until all of them have been touched by the hot butter. Scrape the bottom of the pan well. Douse them with the rest of the lemon juice. Add the chicken, 1/4 cup water, salt, and pepper. Cover and let simmer until the potatoes can mash easily with a fork and the chicken is cooked through. Do not let the mixture get dry. Add more water as needed. Scrape well before serving. Serve hot.

Note: Cook as many potatoes as you think the little ones will eat, because children will ask for more and more.

We are now reaching the end of the liturgical cycle.

Easter being a moveable feast, Lent begins in either February or March, with the ritual cleansing of Clean Monday (instead of Ash Wednesday) for the Orthodox. The Greek Orthodox observe a limited and specific kind of fast—no total abstinence, but avoidance of certain foods, especially meats or dairy, with exceptions on certain of the forty days. Many of the vegetarian dishes in this book are appropriate for observing this fast. After the forty solemn days of Lent, Easter will arrive again, with the promise of resurrection and the renewal of life. Good food and eating together are essential to a happy life.

Kalí órexi, my friends! Enjoy!

Metric Conversion Tables

Metric US Approximate Equivalents

LIQUID INGREDIENTS

METRIC	US MEASURES	METRIC	US MEASURES
1.23 ML	1/4 TSP.	29.57 ML	2 TBSP.
2.36 ML	1/2 TSP.	44.36 ML	3 TBSP.
3.70 ML	3/4 TSP.	59.15 ML	1/4 CUP
4.93 ML	1 TSP.	118.30 ML	1/2 CUP
6.16 ML	1 1/4 TSP.	236.59 ML	1 CUP
7.39 ML	1 1/2 TSP.	473.18 ML	2 CUPS OR 1 PT.
8.63 ML	1 3/4 TSP.	709.77 ML	3 CUPS
9.86 ML	2 TSP.	946.36 ML	4 CUPS OR 1 QT.
14.79 ML	1 TBSP.	3.79 L	4 QTS. OR 1 GAL.

DRY INGREDIENTS

METRIC	US MEASURES	METRIC		US MEASURES
2 (1.8) G	1/16 OZ.	80 G		2 4/5 OZ.
3 1/2 (3.5) G	1/8 OZ.	85 (84.9) G		3 OZ.
7 (7.1) G	1/4 OZ.	100 G		3 1/2 OZ.
15 (14.2) G	1/2 OZ.	115 (113.2) G		4 OZ.
21 (21.3) G	3/4 OZ.	125 G		4 1/2 OZ.
25 G	7/8 OZ.	150 G		5 1/4 OZ.
30 (28.3) G	1 OZ.	250 G		8 7/8 OZ.
50 G	13/4 OZ.	454 G	1 LB.	16 OZ.
60 (56.6) G	2 OZ.	500 G	1 LIVRE	17 3/5 OZ.

Index of Greek Recipe Names

Index of American Recipe Names

About the Author

A native Greek who never lost her connections to her homeland, Katerina Katsarka Whitley is a mother and grandmother, a teacher, a public speaker and dramatist, a writer, a passionate cook, and a cooking instructor. Her freelance writing on Greek culture, food, and travel has appeared in the *News and Observer*, *Catholic Middle East*, *Witness*, and other religious journals, and in the *Christian Science Monitor*, where she also contributed literary essays. In addition to this, she taught at Appalachian State University. Katerina is deeply rooted in her religious community, having worked for over a decade with the Episcopal Church of New York, where she wrote speeches and sermons for bishops and priests. Today, she travels the country as a regular speaker at numerous Episcopal churches.